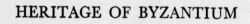

HERITAGE OF BYZANTIUM

HERITAGE OF BYZANTIUM

BY

MARCU BEZA

LONDON

SOCIETY FOR PROMOTING
CHRISTIAN KNOWLEDGE

NORTHUMBERLAND AVENUE, W.C. 2

First published 1947

MADE IN GREAT BRITAIN

CONTENTS

CONTENTS

AUTHOR'S NOTE

THE majority of the following pages appeared first in the national Greek weekly *Hellas*. Gathering them now together in book form, I have to thank the editor of that newspaper, Mr. A. Mitsotakis, not only for allowing me to reprint them, but for the kindness and appreciation with which he always accepted my contribution.

Part of " Orthodoxy in the Balkans " appeared first in *Free Europe*, to the editor of which I also express my thanks.

M. B.

LIST OF ILLUSTRATIONS

PART I
IN SEARCH OF HELLENIC SHRINES

I. ON THE WAY TO BETHLEHEM

NOT yet fully awakened, in a moment of prolonged drow-
siness, I thought to myself, "Where am I?" No sooner
had the question occurred to me than I caught a glimpse
of an ebony crucifix over the doorway leading to the next room.
At the same time, from outside, there reached me the ringing
of a bell, carefully struck as if to avoid disturbing me. Whereupon gentle, feminine voices became audible in the chapel.

"Ah . . . I know. The convent of Tantur, near Jerusalem, on the way to Bethlehem. . . ."

I was sure now. Presently the sun will rise, and I too will
get up and step out on the terrace to feed the birds, as I have
done for a whole week since I arrived here. Innumerable
birds arrived. Seeing how they pecked the crumbs and seeds
thrown to them, I seemed to hear the echo of a Greek song:

> *Upon the endless sea*
> *There is an isle. On the isle*
> *It grows a fairy tree*
> *With all its fruit of gold,*
> *Where birds and birds do gather;*
> *A marvel to behold !*

Mine was a world of enchantment; and I could hardly
believe it, after so many years spent in London, with the
unparalleled din of that immense town, the restlessness and
feverish preoccupations, the benighted discussions at the
clubs. All this now fell below the horizon of my life. When
on the point of moving to Palestine, I said to myself,
"If I go to Jerusalem, the contrast will not be small; I can
establish myself outside, at a monastery, to taste fully the
sense of retirement." I did not regret this decision. The
renewed contact with nature brought under my eyes many
a forgotten friend of childhood: the lady-birds like bits of coral
in the grass; the long rows of ants; the slow-foot tortoises; and
the green and ashen lizards tossing their heads in the sun—
so impressively numerous that I used to meet them in my
dreams. Spellbound, I stopped before the porphyry pome-
granate flowers, avidly I drank in the fine, elusive aroma of the
blossomed olive-trees.

How many things I learnt from my hostesses! Six in number, they spoke, overawed, about their convent's founders, the famous Knights of Malta, of whom one rested undisturbed, illumined by a burning lamp, inside the chapel.

The youngest of the nuns, Sister Valentine, slender of figure, had large, sparkling eyes. As to her hair, I could not say; for she always kept it covered under a thick kerchief. One day, however, a lock of gold escaped on to her shoulder.

"Sister Valentine ! . . ." I exclaimed. She caught the direction of my eyes and hid it, saying abashed:

" I couldn't bear to have my hair cut, because I am still a novice. I didn't put on the ring. Any time I can leave, if I want to."

" And why don't you ?"

" I thought I might get used to the convent, as all the others who are here did."

" But, Sister Valentine, how can you compare yourself ? . . . You are so young and pretty."

She blushed and went quickly, as if not to be overtaken by temptation. In less than a week she came to say goodbye, as she was leaving the convent.

Later on the Abbess Melania, with her severe countenance, let slip many words of blame, ascribing Sister Valentine's conduct to passionate impulses which she, being of weak nature, could not resist. I listened in silence. That same night I found on my bedroom table a few lines from the Abbess Melania:

" I feel I ought not to have spoken as I did about Sister Valentine's departure. Presumably I was wrong in my surmises. God alone can judge and weigh a human soul. We here are rather confused and far from what we really must be. Please forget anything I have said."

When I saw her next, I did not even mention the letter; to avoid embarrassment, I inquired about a miraculous oak-tree found in the vicinity of the convent.

" It's there, quite near," answered the Abbess Melania, " in El-Scharafat village. We might go together."

And so we did one afternoon. We took a footpath to the valley, then climbed, and on the hill-top we heard a flute somewhere ahead—the same few notes were repeated, long-drawn and melancholy, as if it were the complaint of the solitude itself. Soon we detected the flute player, a young Arab, on the outskirts of the village, where the oak-tree rose conspicuously. It stretched its branches to the ground, leaving underneath a wide shelter. The Arab approached us to explain:

" It is sacred. . . . Sick people come to be cured."

" How old could it be ?"

" Who knows ? . . . In a way it was always here. Some time ago it began to wither, which was a heavy grief to us. And what we thought of doing then ! The deep cleft you see on the trunk we filled with cement; we dug holes around and threw stones in them, so that the roots might take some air. And to the great joy of all the tree came again to life."

As we turned towards the convent, there appeared in sight the towers, cupolas and dark cypresses of Jerusalem, all lightly tinged with crimson by the sunset. Thinking of the oak-tree, we fell to conversing about the other oak, that most revered tree of Mamre, where God visited Abraham in the form of celestial messengers. The scene later came to symbolize the Christian Holy Trinity.

Down in front of the Tantur convent runs the road to Bethlehem, trodden once by the Magi. From beyond the Jordan they travelled, and, at a crossing, having lost sight of the star, they went to Jerusalem to question King Herod. The latter, full of doubts, tried to learn of them regarding the birth of the long-looked-for Messiah. Then the Magi departed. On the way, as they rested a moment at a well close by, they saw in the depths of the water the reflection of the missing star. I recited to myself the lines of the Christmas play:

> *We are the Wise Men from the East,*
> *Gaspar and Melchior and Balthazar . . .*

Their strange, remote-sounding names, their gorgeously exotic garments, their rich offerings of gold and spices—all about them has an ever-enduring quality of romance. We owe them, not only the constant appeal they make to the world, but the very existence of the Nativity Church at Bethlehem.

Over its doors there was in old times a mosaic picture— the Adoration of the Magi. Chosroes, the Persian, a reckless destroyer of Christian sanctuaries, saw it when passing through Bethlehem. " The Magi !" he mumbled. "How is it ? The Magi are ours and the star from above. . . . This must be a holy place." And so the church was spared.

Eutychius, a tenth-century Alexandrian Patriarch, left on record that at the beginning the church was built by Constantine; then Justinian pulled it down and erected a larger one. Archæologists were inclined to doubt the story of Eutychius. Soundings made recently, however, inside the church resulted in the discovery of Constantine's ancient pavement with some of the mosaics. These were unexpectedly striking: octagonal-shaped medallions, encompassing ornaments and birds in such lively and free postures; a cock is pecking a bunch of grapes, whilst a partridge stands nearby, undecided. This is choice craftsmanship brought to a high pitch of perfection by Hellenistic art.

II. AT THE MAR-SABA MONASTERY

AFTER three hours' donkey ride from Jerusalem, as I was on the hills above the Dead Sea, I heard the chime of bells coming, as it were, from a long distance.

" They are ringing at the Mar-Saba Monastery," explained my Arab guide. " There, in front of us."

A tower and a strong wall were hardly visible in the reddish colour of the earth. On approaching them a voice called out. My guide replied, and immediately, with the sound of rasping iron, a small gate opened. There was a monk to greet me.

" We knew of your arrival," he said. " The bells are ringing in your honour."

" Thank you, indeed. I never expected it."

He led me downwards to a stone-paved court, and pacing a flight of stairs on the right we entered the refectory, with a large divan on two sides. The monk introduced himself. He was the Prior Agathon, so he told me, hailing from Thessaly, which he had left some thirty years before. I looked at him in wonder. I should have liked to ask what reason had impelled him to forsake a land of woods and cool waters, but he seemed so detached from worldly things that I desisted.

Night descended unexpectedly. Prior Agathon lighted an oil lamp on the table and uttered slowly, " Good evening !" Then he added: " You had better take a rest on the divan here, as we begin the church service rather early—at eleven o'clock."

" Eleven o'clock ? And why so, Father Agathon; why don't you hold service in daytime ?"

" Because it is during the night that the Devil walks about and lays his artful snares. Isn't he called the Prince of Darkness ?"

" I didn't think of that. However, what temptations could there be on your way ? For you do not go out into the world and you do not allow women inside the monastery."

" But, my son, can't one sin also in mind ?"

" Yes, one can, one can. . . ."

As soon as Prior Agathon had gone I stretched myself on the divan and closed my eyes. Some time later I heard in my drowsing the sound of the wood gong—clear, repeated knocks; then many light footsteps. The monks were moving from their cells. Whereupon I got up and followed them into the church.

Before the icons the candles shone like red points of fire through the burning incense. A chanting started, which suddenly for one or two minutes grew very loud, and then subsided into a faint, monotonous, prolonged murmur, until the break of day. Prior Agathon approached me and said:

" Come with us !"

We ascended to the terrace of the monastery, overlooking, as far as I could make out, a steep gorge. Down at its bottom, in the dim light, I could see wild creatures of the desert crawling and eating the food that the monks were now throwing.

" Thus we take care of them every day," spoke Prior Agathon. " They know, and come regularly."

Adding this to the scene I witnessed later—numerous blackbirds with yellowish wings that alighted upon the monks' shoulders and pecked dried figs from their hands—I realized how the need for society prompted the solitary ones to seek the companionship of beasts and fowls, as we often notice in the hagiographies.

Saba the Cappadocian himself is represented with a lion at his feet in the icon that hangs at what used once to form his abode. It might as well have been one of the hermit's caves squeezed in the ravine here. And when Saba decided to establish a monastery, he tried for a better site elsewhere; but the Mother of God appeared to him in a dream and said: " Why dost thou wander in strange paths ? Go back, and thou shalt see fire issuing from a cave, and that shall be to thee a sign where to build. . . ."

It is a fact that the church was cut out beneath a huge rock, in which Prior Agathon's candles brought to light one of the finest Byzantine icons I have gazed upon in Palestine, showing the Ladder of Jacob. In the bright harmony of colours, in the benign angels modelled upon young Byzantine beauties, in the enraptured countenance of the dreamer, in everything it could compare with any of the choicest Renaissance pictures.

At various times holy men from Serbia must have dwelt in Mar-Saba, for otherwise I cannot explain a number of small-sized icons of Serbian origin that are found inside the second, newer church, as well as two Serbian parchment Gospels in excellent script. These, together with other Byzantine relics, we owe entirely to the praiseworthy preservation spirit of the Greek monks.

Between the churches in the court of the monastery, under a chapel dome, lies the tomb of the saintly founder, whose body, however, was long ago carried away by the Crusaders.

And the cloisters—how should I describe them? Balconies, verandahs, and latticed windows seem to hang isolated and haphazard upon the bare surroundings; while amongst them, right and left, up and down, one observes staircases, passages and corridors. At one of the cells I tarried a little. It belonged to St. John the Damascene, greatly to be esteemed, since his actions were entirely in accordance with what he preached in *Barlaam and Joasaph*. At the age of about fifty-five, having disposed of all his possessions and given them to the poor, he retired for good, humble and homeless, to the monastery, where he devoted himself to his priceless meditations and devout hymn-singing.

Close to the cells there extend little gardens—one might call them miniature oases—with grass, flowers, and stunted trees. But, lo! See there! Above all stands a real giant palm. From unfathomable depths it rears its stem, which, with ever-recurring freshness, continues after centuries to bear sweet date-fruit. What amazing vitality! I questioned Prior Agathon: " Have you water ?"

" God has been gracious to us. Once it did not rain for a long time, and the monks suffered. They turned to Saba: ' Do something for us, Holy One !' And he commanded them to fast, to pray for three days and three nights, and thereafter a spring gushed out of the stones."

I hurried to see such a miracle. Eastwards, beneath the monastery's terrace, the water runs in the valley of the feeding beasts. And as I walked through the rocky, apocalyptic scene, by crags and crevices, from whence wild pigeons took their flight in dense clouds, I fell to musing. A wide span of twenty-four centuries separated us from the inmates of the monastery. Theirs was the mentality of the simple ascetic days. Nothing of modern discoveries, or improvements, which we are accustomed to cover under the term of progress, had touched them in the least. That is why we cannot understand them.

And amazing beyond words, indeed, is the thought that during such a tremendous period of time, whilst empires rose to greatness and empires disappeared, life in this desert shrine has gone on almost unchanged, caught in the same routine of the Church—ritual and prayer.

III. GALILEE AND THE HELLENISTIC INFLUENCE
IN PALESTINE

I HALTED again, as I had many times before, at Tabgha, the Greek Eptapegon, meaning Seven Springs, that still run close to where the Hospice now is. A cross on the roof shows its religious character. And what a delightfully soothing place by the Galilean Sea ! The whole of its face is covered with bougainvillea in a dark-blue profusion of flowers. Palm-trees stand guard, while a marble basin with splashing water serves to cool the soft air around.

Resting in the shade and breathing the perfume of oranges, I gazed over the calm azure of Gennesaret. On the right, hardly seen through a haze, Tiberias; on the left, the verdant shores and the Mount of Beatitudes. Nearer, on its slope, there was once to be found a Byzantine church consecrating the spot of the miracle of the Loaves and Fishes. Recent excavations brought its floor to light, with its transepts and with some exquisitely wrought mosaics, the best extant in Palestine.

Within a lotus frame you observe aquatic birds and reeds, papyrus, oleanders, blossomed branches, quite detached, with no roots in land or water. Ducks are perched on stalks, a flamingo at grips with a snake, another dips its beak into the golden cup of a flower. The craftsman's imagination transcends any sense of proportion. He ordains everything towards an artistic whole, to which, desiring likewise to convey an impression of inhabited life, he adds a kiosk here, a tower there, and up in the corner a castle wall.

Caught by the sun, this dream-like picture looks alive, as if the birds are making ready to fly and join their feathered companions on the lake; the cormorants, the grebes, and yet another bird that I have not seen before, of a lustrous turquoise-blue, with white neck and crimson feet, throwing out in passing, short, swift wails as if it were seeking for something.

It is, I learn, the halcyon, which brings serene days around the places where it chooses to build its nest. Did not the Greek poet Alcman sing of it at his old age, when he felt weak and tired of the dancing ?

No more, no honey-sweet voices of love,
Can my limbs carry me; would I were
A halcyon flying on the waves' foam
With no care, sea-purple bird of spring !

I remember, too, that Lucian of Samosata puts in the mouth
of one Chærephon the question:

"What voice was that, Socrates? It reached us from
yonder beach, under the cliff; so pleasant to the ears! Was
it a bird? I thought sea-birds did not sing."

"Indeed, a sea-bird, Chærephon, called the halcyon, full
of moaning and tears; about which a story is left from the old
people."

And Socrates goes on to relate how once the halcyon was a
mortal maiden, daughter of Æolus; how she married the son
of the morning-star, who having perished in far-away lands,
she sought him with piercing cries, even as the halcyon does
to-day, after the gods had changed her into the bird halcyon.

Behold, I think to myself, both Alcman the poet and Lucian
have now been dead for ages, and yet I call them to mind, by
reason of what they left worthy behind them. How more so
with Christ! He embodied the great wealth of His inspiration in a number of expressive sentences which seem to have
been existing for evermore; so profound they are, although
very simple. One feels a joy to repeat them aloud to oneself,
especially in the original Greek. They preserve the same
freshness as in the days when they were uttered.

It is true the fair Galilean cities of that time no longer exist.
The wind of perdition has passed through them. Sunk into
the dust are Magdala and Eptapegon and Bethsaida. Nothing
remains of Gadara, where Meleager the poet kept one of the
last candles alight to Hellenism. The black tents of the
Bedouins spread over the cities of Capernaum and Chorazin.
Only by chance their ruined synagogues present us with some
lions and vultures carved in stone, testifying to the strong
Greek influence, of which we catch a glimpse in the beginning
of St. John's Gospel.

Centuries before and after the advent of Christ the intellectual
class in Palestine made use of Greek. And in Greek are most
of the inscriptions on tombs, from Galilee down to Beit Gibrin,
which might be called a region of the dead. Its surrounding
hills, such as Tell El-Judeideh and Tell Sandahannah, consist
of innumerable caves hewn out of the limestone, with labyrin-
thine corridors and sepulchral chambers, the most remarkable
and richly decorated being here the tomb of one Apollo-
phanes of Marissa.

In the shape of a chapel, its inner recess for burials divided
from the outer space by a door, it bears on the right hand of
the latter the Greek inscription:

Οὐκ ἔχω τί σοι πάθω ἢ τὶ χαρίσω μαι, κατακεῖμαι μεθ' ἑτέρου σὲ
μέγα φιλοῦσα.
'Αλλὰ νὴ τὴν 'Αφροδίτην μέγα τι χαίρω, ὅτι σοῦ τὸ ἱμάτιον
ἐνέχυρα κεῖται.
'Αλλ' ἐγὼ μὲν ἀποτρέχω, σοὶ δὲ καταλείπω εὐρυχωρίαν πολλήν,
πρᾶσσε, ὅτι βούλει.
Μὴ κροῦε τὸν τοῖχον, ψόφος ἐγγίνεται, ἀλλὰ διὰ τῶν θυρῶν
(π)νεύμασι κεῖται.

These four lines, written by different hands, scatter like
sunbeams the time-gathered shadows and illumine for us a
distant episode of everyday humanity. There once lived two
lovers, Myron and Calypso. In want of a more suitable place,
they secretly met at the tomb-chamber and talked their hearts
out to each other, as lovers always did.

But it so happened that Calypso's parents had no liking for
Myron, and married her to another man. And Calypso,
wishing to explain things to her lover, unable to see him,
hurried to the place where they used to meet, and there traced
upon the wall what she wanted Myron to know:

> *There is nothing I would not suffer for thee or wherein please thee.*
> *I lie with another, though I love thee greatly.*

Myron did come and read this, but he reacted as Calypso
never would have expected. Jealousy turned his love into
bitter hatred and venom. And so he wrote under Calypso's
lines:

> *But by Aphrodite! Of one thing I am very glad, that thy cloak*
> *lieth in pawn.*

It meant that, being in possession of her cloak, he could
contrive and work a dreadful charm against Calypso, who,
overwhelmed with fright and grief, took a sudden resolution:

> *But I run away, and leave thee much freedom,*
> *Do whatever thou wilt.*

The words implied far more than their simple sense. For
another person, identifying himself with one of the dead in the
adjoining room, added the remark:

> *Do not strike the wall; it makes a noise;*
> *Through the doors she lieth—with ghosts.*

Indeed, with ghosts; where no harm could reach Calypso any
longer. And then? What about Myron? What had Calypso's own husband to say? We do not know. The shadows
fall heavy again. And we are inclined to whisper the words of
Hamlet: 　　　　　　　*The rest is silence.*

IV. THE SOURCES OF ADONIS

NOT far from Byblos, turning to a sidewalk, I caught a full view of the snow-clad mountain.

" That's Lebanon," said my guide, stretching out his hand. " Up there, near the village of Afka, are the sources of Adonis."

And I proceeded upon the undulating hills, covered mostly by old knotty mulberry-trees. Here I got away from, and here I approached the river, called to-day Nahr-Ibrahim, which flickers, lost in deep and dizzy precipices. Different, more direct, must once have been the sacred way followed by the festive processions. Starting from Byblos they used to halt at special places where hymns were sung and episodes from the life of the god dramatically represented. Upon some rocks Adonis himself is still shown with raised spear waiting the onslaught of the death-bringing boar. The tragic end of the hero threw a shadow over the whole district. From his blood grew red anemones, the face of the river was empurpled, the women of Lebanon wept uncomforted.

After three hours I reach the village of Afka with a little white church in the centre and a few scattered huts. I fancy myself at the end of the world. There in front descend stony, sheer mountain flanks, shadowing and guarding the river which springs from the widely yawning mouth of a cave. I pass in with torches and penetrate deep through galleries and corners of incessant night. Startled by the smoking flare of the torches swarms of bats flutter around. I look in vain for inscriptions. But here and there I notice terraces, vaults and niches which testify to the care of human hands. Presumably they served for the performance of the orgiastic Mysteries so bitterly denounced by the Fathers of the Church.

Falling in cascades, the river presently flows peacefully into a pool. There lie, partly in water, the foundations of the temple of Astarte. I walk at random through its ruins that are heaped around. Somewhere I pick up an old coin. It is rusty. I can only make out two or three letters, and the head of a king—palpable sign, however, of the life that once existed here. And there passed over it earthquakes and ordeals of fanaticism, without quenching in the least the profound human thirst for believing in something which seems to change but

23

essentially remains the same. For in a hollow of the ancient wall people still to this day light candles and burn spices. And from the branches of a fig-tree nearby there hang innumerable offerings—ribbons, pieces of cloth, handkerchiefs, many-coloured rags. I feel as if I ought to kneel down myself and pray.

MARBLE SCULPTURED VULTURES, SYNAGOGUE OF CAPERNAUM

ANGELS CONTENDING WITH DEMONS FOR THE SOUL OF A MAN;
ICON, MAR=SABA MONASTERY

(Facing p. 24)

FIG-TREE WITH OFFERINGS AT THE SOURCES OF ADONIS

ENTRANCE TO HELLENISTIC TOMB

V. FAMAGUSTA

IT is called in Greek Ammochostos, which means sunk in the sand. Nothing could describe it better. Sand coloured are its wall fortifications, with parapets, ramparts, and a dry, wide moat; the city itself within looks no less sand coloured. And all seems very quiet—the bazaar, the shops, the little cafés.

Humble people linger noiselessly, ghost-like, in the shimmering, warm sunlight. From time to time a few camels, remnants as it were of broken-up caravans, pass by, leaving sounds of bells behind them which soon die away.

Against this setting there loom aspects of an alien, superimposed life: on the seashore the citadel tower where Othello writhed furiously in his jealousy, and many Gothic churches scattered through the town, of which the most important in its medieval dignity is that of St. Nicholas, with massive round columns, stone lace-worked windows and triple-arched doors.

A few yards away, utterly ruined, lies the residence of the Cypriot rulers, who used to bear the fictitious crown of Jerusalem's kings. In this oppressingly calm centre who could imagine the throb, the feverish bustle of a city that found itself unexpectedly abounding in riches?

For on the fall of Acre in 1291 many Crusade leaders, with large retinues and newly obtained high-sounding titles, entered Famagusta. To Famagusta were transferred the principal banks and business houses of Venetians, Genoese and Persians.

And Famagusta, raised to the rank of an emporium for the entire Levant world, hummed with every tongue and creed. Its galleys discharged the far-off exotic merchandise, and went out loaded with silks, exquisite Lefcara laces, luscious wines, and aromatic oils and perfumes.

But money thus amassed, for the sake of money, with the sole purpose of seeking worldly pleasures, lust and luxury, where else could it lead than to whimsically insane ideas, such as the taming of leopards for the chase and the dyeing of horses' and dogs' tails in orange or red?

At times, quite suddenly, like an icy cold wind, some dreadful prophecy about the approaching Last Judgment or some threatening call to repentance swept over the city. Then business men and courtesans alike paused, and thought to atone for their sins by building churches. But soon they reverted to their sybaritic rejoicing, revels and wanton processions, in which the Lusignan kings shared not a little.

They were a feudal dynasty, lasting for about three centuries in Cyprus, and reaching their climax under Peter I, that knight-errant who matched his religious zeal with an equal cruelty and debauchery. Both Froissart and Philippe de Mézières relate what they knew of him, his indefatigable efforts towards a new crusade; whilst a side of his intimate life entered into the making of a Greek Cypriot poem, *The Song of the Queen and Arodafnusa*—by the latter is meant Jeanne l'Aleman, the mistress of Peter I, " King of the East and Monarch of the West." It describes for us the meeting of the two rival women:

" Greeting to you, Queen, Daughter of Kings !" Thus Arodafnusa addresses the Queen, who as a sign of welcome presents her with a chemise of gold. The enamoured King, relieved in mind, and gay, speaks:

" The Queen has roses, caskets of jewels, what does she desire ?"

" To see you, talk to you, walk with you," answers the Queen.

Then she takes Arodafnusa by the hand and leads her into the garden, as though the two of them were sisters. The slaves rejoice. A pleasant day passes, and the sun goes down. Arodafnusa says to the Queen:

" I did not come to amuse myself, but in obedience to a command. Permit me to wish you a long life."

The Queen appears not to hear her, but in a low voice:

" Tell me, who is the beloved of the King of the East and Monarch of the West ?"

" I cannot tell you, Queen. I—I do not know—— " falters Arodafnusa, and quickly begins to descend the staircase backwards.

Ultimately the Queen shuts her up in a convent at Famagusta.

It is a relief passing from this turbid past to the nearby site of Salamis, a name savouring of glory that sends one's thoughts back to the Trojan times. One of the heroes, Teucer, wandering on many seas, arrived at the Egyptian island of Pharos. He wanted to inquire of the prophetess Theonoe how to reach Cyprus, where Apollo bade him rear a new city and call it Salamis in memory of his own country left behind:

οὖ μ' ἐθέσπισεν
οἰκεῖν Ἀπόλλων, ὄνομα νησιωτικὸν
Σαλαμῖνα θέμενον τῆς ἐκεῖ χάριν πάτρας.

So Euripides tells us in his strange play, *Helen*. And in time Teucer did rear Salamis, near the unchanged turquoise-blue sea, reflecting a no less beautiful sky.

The city to-day is overgrown with thickets. Its unearthed agora and white marbles speak of the ancient greatness. Excavations, however, brought to light here far more remnants relative to the early Christian world. And no wonder, for it was to Salamis that Paul and Barnabas undertook one of the first missionary journeys; witness the Acts of the Apostles, " And coming to Salamis they preached the word of God in the synagogue of the Jews. . . ."

Hence the strong Christian spirit pervading Cyprus, and particularly Salamis. Here in Salamis Saint Catherine started her devout life; later on she suffered martyrdom at Alexandria. Her body was miraculously carried on to Mount Sinai, and buried there at the monastery. In the flower of youth, urged to marriage by her parents, she went to seek advice from a hermit at Salamis. He said to her:

" I know of only one, wise, learned and full of all gifts such as you would desire."

" Who is he, good father ?"

" Our Lord Jesus Christ."

" Then I wish Him as my bridegroom and master."

And the same night an angel descended from heaven and gave the virgin Catherine the ring of her union with Jesus.

It was again a bishop of Salamis, Epiphanius, who as early as the fourth century won the distinction of being an ardent debater in books like *Panaria* and *Ancoratus*, containing much valuable ecclesiastical information.

A native of Salamis happened to be Barnabas himself, who met his death at Salamis for preaching Christianity. A Byzantine white church close to Salamis is dedicated to him. Inside it one of the frescoes—copy of that discovered in the Cathedral of Nicosia—unfolds pictorially an old traditional episode.

It is the year of our Lord 477. In a dream Barnabas reveals to the Bishop of Salamis, Anthenias, the place of his tomb, unknown till then. And we see how Anthenias, with people and clergy, digs up the coffin; and, behold, he finds in it a Gospel of St. Matthew written by the very hand of Barnabas. Such a precious relic is worthy, no doubt, of Byzantium.

And thither goes Anthenias, presenting it to the Emperor
Zeno, who, very gratified, places a purple cloak upon Anthenias's shoulders. Furthermore, he adds to the gift a sceptre
instead of the usual staff, and grants Anthenias the exceptional
rights of signing in red ink—all these being symbols of the full
Church independence in Cyprus.

VI. APHRODITE IN CYPRUS

FROM the summit of Mount Troados I had a bird's-eye view of Cyprus, placed by a kind destiny amidst the emerald waters on the cross-ways of two continents. After passing through Famagusta with its impressive contrast between a Levantine background and Gothic monuments, and through Nicosia, rich in memorials of the Crusades, I proceeded to ancient Paphos. The city's history goes back to pre-Trojan times, for Agamemnon himself had received the gift of a breast-plate from the Paphian King Kiniras. Was the temple then in existence ?

Its famous goddess came from distant Sumeria, where Tammuz trod the nether realms of darkness and returned anew to the light of day, attracted and cherished by Astarte. The same divine pair, changed into Osiris and Isis, were worshipped, now with laments and anon with joyful songs, along the Nile. And of Tammuz likewise, named by the Phœnicians Adonis, the fire-like anemones and the crimsoned river coming down from Lebanon bore witness. His beloved Astarte crossed over and introduced her own worship into Cyprus.

But here the Greeks, with their æsthetic sense and gift of imagination, had conceived her as a full-grown figure springing white from the white sea-foam; hence Aphrodite, a symbol of perfect beauty. Does not this mean that a real work of art, no matter how much toil enters into its making, should give the impression of spontaneity, as if it had happened of itself and had caught within it something of the miraculously ever-enduring spirit ?

Pygmalion in his artistic frenzy fell madly in love with a statue created by his own hands, to which Aphrodite gave the breath of life. Out of this union Paphos came into the world. And Paphos it was who raised the temple upon a height in sight of the sea, with its cool groves laid out in terraces, its marbled porticoes, its sacred tripods, and a statue of the goddess instead of the ancient cone; with young priestesses in loose, glittering veils; with portent-bearing white flights of doves. Of such famed splendour only a few inscribed stones and fragments of walls remain to mark for us the site of the temple, where to-day the village of Kouklia is found.

No longer does the altar smoke with incense and aromatic

herbs; no longer sounds the rhythm of the mystic dances; no longer do worshippers from afar disembark, drawn by the lure of the chorus in Euripides' *Bacchæ*:

ἐκεῖ χάριτες, ἐκεῖ πόθος. . . .

There are delights, there is desire. . . .

None the less, the goddess still keeps a hold on the minds of the people. In the midst of the ruined temple there is a chapel inside with an image of the Virgin Mary, called the Aphroditissa. To the Virgin Mary a church is also consecrated at the sea-shore; and yet another church quite near, known as " Panaghia i Theoskepastos "—Most Holy One, covered by God—for she was enveloped in a cloud and was not to be seen in time of danger.

On the road to New Paphos one descends into an enclosure, where among faded wall-paintings one again comes across an image of the Virgin Mary under the name of Solomoni. The branches of a huge tree nearby are laden with coloured threads, ribbons, bits of linen—offerings of the devout.

Everywhere the Holy Virgin in full pagan beauty has replaced Aphrodite, so much bound to the mountains, woods and rivers of Cyprus. I thought particularly of the celebrated Fountain of Love. Vaguely I knew that it was towards Acamas, on the west of the island, close to Neochori. I asked two old men:

" Fountain of Love ? " they said. " Never heard of it. You mean, perhaps, the Aphrodite's Bath."

" What is that like ? "

From their description I realized that it was what I sought. Forward I went, alongside a pure sapphire sea. After a time I heard the sound of babbling water. Whole bushes of white-flowered myrtles and oleanders with great blossoms appeared; intoxicating perfumes hung in the air.

A little further on a hollowed rock was revealed, out of which grew fig-trees, spreading themselves above it and thus deepening the rock's shadow. The water flowed from many places: in full streams, in little trickles, in a continual splash of drops—it flowed, chanting a vivid spell, and ran into the crystal pool below.

The sun's rays shyly penetrated, trembled, and shone upon the grass and lichen on the rocky walls. It was, indeed, more than a fountain; it was a true Bath of Aphrodite. It has passed into legend as a miracle of strength and inspiration for

lovers. Poets have sung its praises from hearsay, never having
seen it. And behold, I have come and have drunk eagerly of
its water, and have reached the verdant bed where once rested
her adored body, stirrer of passion and amorous vigils.

Glory be to you, O Goddess Aphrodite ! If, as I think, you
have not entirely withdrawn from these haunts of yours, if there
is still potency in the magic of your well, keep in me untouched
the flame of love and perpetual wonder, and grant that,
absorbing into myself all the loveliness that is in the world, I
may rise to the contemplation of your divine and imperishable
beauty !

VII. PATMOS AND THE APOCALYPSE

PATMOS is one of the so-called Dodecanese Islands in the Ægean Sea. One can reach it by way of Rhodes in a few hours. From afar can be seen the monastery of St. John the Divine rising up on the hill. The harbour of La Scala is dominated by the new Government House. Close by, in the piazza, a fountain stands under green shadows. Midway from here to the monastery, and on the left side of a steep road there is the grotto, where, according to tradition, St. John wrote the Apocalypse. As I passed it, I said to myself, "First I'll go to see the monastery and then come down here."

The brilliantly white houses of the village huddle together round the monastery. In the narrow streets I met groups of boys singing from house to house of the arrival of St. Basil. I then remembered that it was New Year's Eve and that I too, as a boy, had sung the same Greek song:

> *Saint Basil is coming,*
> *Coming along from Caesarea . . .*

I entered the open court of the monastery through a large gate; porticoes and cistern are on one side of the court. The columns, arcades and walls are all whitewashed, save for a small portion left to its own brownish colour—evidence of a remote past. For the monastery dates from the year 1088 when Alexis Comnenus I granted Patmos to St. Christodulos, in order to build the monastery on it; and one can still see in its library the beautifully ornate golden bull of the emperor.

I was received very courteously by the Superior of the monastery. It then being the hour of Vespers, he invited me to the holy service. In the entrance of the church lies a rich coffin containing the embalmed body of St. Christodulos, the founder of the monastery. As on the eve of other festive days, prayers were offered for the souls of the long-departed benefactors of the monastery. In the recital of names I caught some which were familiar to me.

Next day many of the island's notabilities forgathered in the refectory, and in a fitting, solemn manner the Abbot cut the customary cake of St. Basil. As the wine-glasses passed from hand to hand, we fell to talking of the bygone days when Patmos was infested by pirates. The monks of those

ICON OF THE VIRGIN MARY APHRODITISSA, PAPHOS

(Facing p. 32)

PATMOS MONASTERY WITH THE VILLAGE AROUND

BELLS OF PATMOS MONASTERY

(Facing p. 33)

times kept incessant watch on the terrace of the monastery; when they scented any danger, they gave warning and the whole village hurried within its fortified walls. That is why it presents the aspect of a medieval castle rather than that of a monastery.

One of the monks conducted me to St. John's cave, under a chapel which stretched along the slope of the hill. The obscurity here is relieved by an ever-burning lamp. Pointing to a crevice in the rock of the cave, the monk said: " You see, it split when that thunderous voice came to St. John from above: ' I am Alpha and Omega, the first and the last ' . . . "

The cave's mouth opens towards the sea. I gaze reflectively around. Both the water and the sky are of an exquisite blue; the hills appear barren, indeed, but their outlines are gentle and clearly defined. There is nothing vague or hazy in the atmosphere. Wherefrom did St. John get those tremendous visions that throng the pages of the Apocalypse? His mind was wholly steeped in Hebrew apocalypse and prophecies. Upon them he modelled his own inspiration, presenting even verbal similarities.

The four beasts of Daniel's Book became the attributes of a single one in the Apocalypse:

" And the beast which I saw was like unto a leopard, and his feet were as the feet of a boar, and his mouth as the mouth of a lion." St. John begins the same chapter, XIII:

" And I stood upon the sand of the sea, and saw a beast rise up out of the sea, having seven heads and ten horns and upon his horns ten crowns, and upon his heads the name of blasphemy." And the chapter ends:

" Here is wisdom. Let him that hath understanding count the number of the beast; for it is the number of a man: and his number is Six hundred three-score and six."

Christian interpreters, not knowing what to make of all this, looked for hidden meanings. As the Apocalypse was written soon after the death of Nero and as there persisted a strange rumour that the Roman emperor had not really died, that people had seen him in Athens, they thought, to whom else but to him could the words of the Apocalypse refer—" the beast that was and is not and yet is "? Such a belief gathered additional strength from the fact that 666 of the beast corresponds to the numerical value of the letters comprised in the name of the emperor, *Neron Kaisar* spelt in Hebrew *Nron Ksr*.

The truth is, the Apocalypse, though in Greek, through it, construction and style attaches itself to the Hebrew literatures which in its own way is impressive, but it lacks that measured simplicity of the Hellenes.   And the Church Fathers, who were under the overwhelming spell of Plato and the Greek trage- dians, could not take much interest in the Apocalypse.   For this reason one hardly finds any Byzantine artistic representa- tions inspired by the Apocalypse previous to the fifteenth century.   All that seems to have been derived from it, up till then, are the vowels A and Ω, often seen alone or on either side of the sacred Byzantine monogram; and also the Apoca- lyptic animals Man, Lion, Ox and Eagle, found also in Ezekiel, which came to symbolize the four Evangelists.

It was later, when Byzantium broke down, that the Eastern Christian readers and artists turned to the Apocalypse.

One reads in chronicles about the Moldavian prince, Stephen the Great, how he many a time used to ask for the Superior of a monastery to come and explain passages of the Apocalypse. With deep awe the latter read out:

" And I saw the beast and the Kings of the earth and their armies gathered together to make war against him that sat on the horse and against his army.   And the beast . . ."

Prince Stephen enquired in wonder who the beast might be.

On this account, Prince Stephen held the Patmos monastery in great veneration, and endowed it with a number of precious gifts, including a finely embroidered chasuble and a pair of liturgical fans in gold filigree, dated 1488. The donation charter of the monastery by another prince displays in its coloured initial letter the eagle of the Apocalypse.

Connected with the monastery there came into being in Patmos a Greek school of high renown, destined to exercise not a little influence upon Eastern Orthodoxy. Its founder, Macarius Kaloghera, studied in Constantinople and enjoyed the protection of the Mavrocordatos; which is responsible for a manuscript in the monastery, dated 1707, and inscribed:

" My property, Nicolas Mavrocordatos. . . ."

Another manuscript of the monastery, containing counsels to the Jews, refers likewise to a member of the same family:

" They were made clear by the command of His Highness Constantin Nicolas Mavrocordatos."

Amongst the prominent pupils of the Patmos school must be mentioned Monach Daniel, teacher in the houses of Ipsilanti and Kallimachi; and Daniel Pantuva, Metropolitan of Sebastia, who sent to the Patmos monastery a Holy Gospel with richly ornamented covers, bearing the inscription:

" Bequeathed to the venerable Apocalypse Monastery of John the Theologian by the humble Metropolitan of Sebastia."

One of the learned men associated in those days with the Phanariote princes, Maximos the Peloponnesian, bethought himself of giving an illuminated Apocalypse, of which a copy was discovered in 1932 by Miss Elizabeth Day McCormick and published by the University of Chicago Press. To the author of this codex the Apocalyptic beast, identified long before with Antichrist, stood for the Head of the people who were then dominating the Balkans.

VIII. A JOURNEY TO PAROS

THE mere utterance of the name Paros is apt to evoke before one's eyes white-marbled statues. On the approach to the island its capital, Parechia, wears likewise a white-marbled appearance, and the same occurs in regard to numerous windmills which turn and turn around, touched by the sea breeze.

Passing, then, from the full sunny harbour to the town itself, what a pleasant sensation ! The streets are cool and narrow. The house-balconies stretch forward, so much so that persons on opposite sides might shake hands with each other.

As I arrive from the incessant din and restlessness of a great city, I am deeply conscious of and much welcome the quiet of Parechia. It descends upon me like a heavenly benediction. When I begin to wander about, when I enter the secluded courtyards or walk out under green awnings of vines, whose leaves rustle in my ears, when I breathe the soft air laden with mingled aromas of laurels and oranges, when I catch now and again distant glimpses of glittering turquoise bays, I feel that these are indeed unforgettable impressions.

Talking to one or other of the people, I hear about Nicolas Mavrogheni, how much they cherish and keep his memory alive, on account of the great benefits he had bestowed on the island. It speaks well for the character of this Prince that, when he reached a high social position, he turned his careful attention to the place of his descent.

He knew that Parechia was suffering from scarcity of water. Therefore, he caused a number of small mountain springs to be drawn into a basin, called to the present day the " Princely Source." Thence, through pipes, the water was brought down to the town, where he built three marble fountains, all in ornamented Turkish style.

Under a Greek appropriate stanza, making the fountain itself call:

Come you all in multitudes to me,
Take, and quench your thirst, and then depart !

one sees a cross between the christian and family name:

NICOLAS MARVROGHENIS

After the fountains had been erected in 1777, the Prince

bethought himself of paving the streets of Parechia with stones and lavishing his varied kind of help on the Assumption of Virgin Mary's Monastery; most renowned this throughout the Cyclades as Ekatondapyliani, that is, the Monastery of the Hundred Gates. No doubt it dates from the Byzantine days, and there entered into its construction many a remnant of the old temples. The principal church entrance shows on either side the figure in marble of a man crushed under the pressure of heavy columns.

" Who is he ?" I inquired.

" The master-builder. They put him to death lest he would have raised another church as lofty as this one."

One meets here with a legend of Eastern origin, used, too, by James Elroy Flecker in his play *Hassan*. When the hero expresses his admiration:

" What a beautiful fountain, with the silver dolphin and the naked boy !"

Answers the Caliph Haroun Al Raschid:

" A Greek of Constantinople made it, who came travelling hither in the days of my father, the Caliph El Mahdi—may earth be gentle to his body and Paradise refreshing to his soul ! He showed this fountain to my father, who was exceptionally pleased, and asked the Greek if he could make more as fine. ' A hundred,' replied the delighted infidel. Whereupon my father cried, ' Impale the pig.' Which, having been done, this fountain remains the loveliest in the world."

A variant in the Balkans tells about the master-builder being left to end his days on the top of the church just finished. What was he to do ? An idea struck him as the only hope in moments of despair. He fashioned a pair of wooden wings according to his own device. When he attempted to fly, however, like Icarus of yore, he fell and crashed to the ground.

The Church of Ekatondapyliani is high and spacious inside. And I am glad to find that the wall-paintings in the chancel are well preserved under a white layer of gypse, which, taken out, they will again glow and reveal their original freshness, as it happened with St. Sophia's mosaics in Istanbul.

A most elaborately carved, four-pillared iconostas bears on its centre the fitting inscription out of Virgin Mary's Acathist:

Χαῖρε, ὅτι ὑπάρχεις Βασιλέως καθέδρα,
Χαῖρε, ὅτι βαστάζεις τὸν βαστάζοντα πάντας.

Hail, for thou art the throne of a King,
Hail, for thou carriest the carrier of all !

Underneath three large-sized icons—they are conspicuous—
one representing Our Lady with Christ in her arms; the second,
a nimbed Christ; the third, the Assumption of the Virgin Mary.
Of excellent Byzantine craftsmanship, adorned with gold and
silver and precious stones; they all display the Princely emblem
of the donor, Nicolas Mavrogheni.

Furthermore, I read in a codex of the church: " Seven holy
vestments, being the gift of His Highness Nicolas Mavrogheni,
were sent and received here, the year 1786." I mention from
amongst these, still extant, a heavy phelon in gold, and a stole
with embroidered evangelists and vine decoration.

Only such specimens of ecclesiastical art can Paros show
nowadays to visitors. For any ancient relics she possessed, any
sculptured deities, any mortal forms moulded in the brilliance
of her immortal marble had all gone. Like other Greek islands,
cities and monasteries, Paros, too, had not been spared by that
rapacious tribe of antique and manuscript hunters.

IX. THE MONASTERIES OF MOUNT ATHOS

FROM Salonica, where I spent the bygone years of child-hood, my father often went on business to Mount Athos. On his return home he always had many tales to tell. With haste and joyous impatience I drew near him, listening to his voice, which now and again dropped and deepened into the revelation of isolated shrines where only the tired steps of the pilgrims passed, of hermits concealed in caves, of great bells beyond compare that rang suddenly by themselves, of wonder-working icons. And the things father brought with him! Dishes of carved wood, little crucifixes with specks of glass, ivory amulets, rosaries of amber. How marvellous were all these to me !

Therefore, one will realize that I felt not a little moved when my eyes first gazed upon Athos. There rose, straight, marmoreal, the mountain of my cherished memories to which now was added the knowledge I had gathered about it from various ancient authors. Especially I called to mind the lines of Æschylus in *Agamemnon*, when Clytemnestra speaks of the beacons announcing the fall of Troy. Hephæstus sent the fire message which

> *Ida first*
> *To Lemnian Rock of Hermes flung,*
> *And third from the island was caught*
> *By the lofty Athos of God Zeus. . . .*

> Ἴδη μὲν πρὸς Ἑρμαῖον λέπας
> Λῆμνον· μέγαν δὲ πανὸν ἐκ νήσου τρίτον
> Ἄθωον αἶπος Ζηνὸς ἐξεδέξατο. . . .

It is to be noticed that Æschylus gives Athos the epithet Ζηνὸς, pertaining to Zeus, divine; at least so it was believed. There always clung to it a certain awe. Four years after the advent of Christianity, Arcadius—the son of the Byzantine Emperor Theodosius—happened to be shipwrecked. The Virgin Mary went to his rescue, and, having brought him safely to Athos, she said:

" Let no woman henceforth set her foot on this holy soil !"

It was thus the Blessed Mary herself who allotted Mount Athos to men, whom neither woman nor anything reminding of woman should lead into temptation. And from an early time did such seekers after seclusion begin to arrive hither, as is confirmed by an old codex, Ἱστορικὸς Λόγος of Kostamoni-tou, which asserts that prior to the existence of monasteries, during the Iconoclastic period between 717-843, the anchorites of Mount Athos were striving to Christianize the wandering shepherds.

They lived separately, meeting only on special occasions. When their number increased, naturally they had to come under the head of one called Protos, First, whose own rights and rela-tions to others were regulated by a Chrysobul of Leo the Philosopher in 911. About fifty years later Nicephorus Phocas entrusted Athanasius, a friend of the days when he was not yet Emperor, with the task of building the great Lavra. Subse-quently the other monasteries were founded, twenty in all.

Amongst them in the centre there grew up a village by the name of Karyes, whose medieval aspect has remained un-changed up to the present day. I recognized it from my father's description. Here I found the skilfully wrought things of my childhood, glittering in the shadow of little shops, within which moved pale young monks. Here quiet reigned, not a tremor of love, not a whisper of the other sex. Furthermore, here one was not allowed to ride, neither to sing nor smoke.

From Karyes I proceeded to visit the monasteries. On path-ways I went, amidst a scenery abounding in beauties—hazels mingled with laurels, chestnuts with orange-trees, while vines threw their rich laceries on the boughs.

The porch of Vatopedi's Church shows in its frescoes, side by side with saints, the figures of Aristotle, Plato, Æschylus, Sophocles and others, which means that the Christian Fathers considered ancient Greek writers as forerunners of Christ.

As the Esphigmenou Monastery has direct access to the sea its inmates indulge in fishing. When they bring in the catch a bell rings. The cats know this particular sound, and rush to the shore, hundreds of them. I inquired, amazed: " How is it there are so many ? Where do they come from ?"

The answer was: " What can we do ? They conduct their amours and multiply in the forest."

At Iviron one day the monks saw an icon of the Virgin Mary arriving miraculously from the seas. In its honour they erected a chapel, where to this day the icon is worshipped.

Over St. Simion's tomb at Chilandari there grows a vine from which the grapes are very propitious to suckling mothers.

A story centres around Caracalla. One of the rich and pious princes from beyond the Danube sent his greatest dignitary to build the monastery, providing him with the needed funds. With part of these he raised a tower; the rest he kept for himself.

When the prince heard of it, he ordered his execution, but the dignitary fell on his knees and prayed to be spared. He solemnly promised to build the monastery, which he did. Soon afterwards both he and the prince took the vows, under the same name of Pachomius. They are portrayed at the entrance of Caracalla's Church in the black habit of monks. The inscription reads:

Οἱ νέοι κτήτορες τῆς ἁγίας μονῆς ταύτης Παχώμιος καὶ Παχώμιος.

The new founders of this saintly monastery, Pachomius and Pachomius.

Along with such features of the monasteries there goes a variety of types. It takes all kinds to make an Athonite community, which is a world unto itself. Some entered the Holy Mount as little boys, without leaving it since; they are not aware of how a woman looks in reality. Others embraced monasticism at a mature age, in order to atone for sins which burdened their souls.

Others, simple-minded, believed that the mere fact of passing their earthly days in Athos would secure for them the perpetual felicity of the hereafter. Feeling rather unwell one day, I said to the Abbot of a monastery: " I am ill, Father. I think I shall leave my bones on Mount Athos." He consoled me: " What luck that would be for you, my son, to die here ! You would go straight into Paradise." And there are not a few honestly addicted to contemplation and studies.

As for the appearance of the monasteries, it is indeed striking. Unexpectedly they emerge, as it were, up on the heights, huge and massive, with their battlements, towers and projected balconies, one above the other. You would think them fairy castles. This is the impression which persists also in their interiors.

Their treasure houses are in the custody of three monks, each with his own key. One comes and opens a heavy iron door. You enter. Another steps in with a key fitted to the lock of the second door. There follows a third similar door. Only then do you find yourself face to face with undreamt-of relics.

And here lies the great merit of Mount Athos—to have preserved for us a number of characteristically rare specimens of Byzantine art, such as, for instance, the golden triptych, comprising a cross set with jewels, presented to Lavra by the Emperor Nicephorus Phocas; the beautiful chalice of Manuel Paleologus at Vatopedi; the twelfth-century Gospel in golden letters on white parchment, a remarkable gift of Andronicus Comnenus to Chilandari; the richly adorned Slavonic Gospel, brought by Robert Curzon to the British Museum from Saint Paul's Monastery, bearing an inscription to the effect that once it was pawned and that a Moldavian prince redeemed it in the sixteenth century.

On the other hand, Mount Athos afforded ample opportunity to various artists for expressing themselves in the work done at Lavra, Protatou, Vatopedi, Xenophontos, Chilandari, Dionysiou, Docheariou. The paintings, untarnished in their splendour, are associated with famous names, such as Manuel Panselinos, Theophanes and others.

Whether belonging to the Macedonian or Cretan schools, they infused Byzantine art with a new breath, fresh and stirring like a springtime breeze. It is of late, in such books as *The Birth of Western Paintings* by R. Byron and D. Talbot Rice, that one comes to realize the Byzantine influences of the Athonite kind over Europe, through painters like El Greco.

Besides, Mount Athos evolved a style of its own. Upon a liturgical fan, given to Patmos by the Moldavian prince Stephen the Great, we read the words:

" It was made at Zographou Monastery of the Great Martyr George in Mount Athos, 1488."

This obviously explains that some of the monks harboured in the monasteries were real craftsmen, and they professed to be such, accepting pupils who, formed under their guidance, went elsewhere, in the neighbouring countries, to spread the benefit of their talents.

So, nowadays, the minute carvings in wood, the filigree bowls, the crosses of intricate workmanship, the silver discs, the ornamented lamps, the small icons—all such objects we see and prize much throughout the Balkans—are to be traced mostly to Mount Athos, which always stood as a worthy symbol of Eastern Orthodoxy's achievement in art.

X. PRELUDE TO GREEK INDEPENDENCE

ASCENDING the hills beyond Volos one enters a region apart, stretched, as it were, under a golden haze of legends. One's fancy goes back to the far-off days of Achilles and the wondrous quest of the Argonauts. The villages have something remote, unspoiled by any modern trivialities. I am sorry to be able to do no more than pass through them, for my goal is Zagorà.

It befell that a native of that town, Bishop Kalinic, for a short time Patriarch in 1757, bequeathed his whole library to it. No less generous was he towards the church of St. George, quaint in appearance, adorned inside by a richly carved wood pulpit and episcopal throne. I am at a loss to explain how it came to be there—a superb antiminsion in bronze, made at Moschopoli for presentation, as the inscription reveals, to the Holy Sepulchre.

By a stroke of luck I found Rhiga Pheraios' map of Moldavia in the library. Its existence had only been assumed; another map by Rhiga Pheraios, the one of Wallachia, had been well known. The latter bore on it the portrait of Alexander Ypsilanti, the former that of Alexander Mavrocordato, called Phiraris, because he fled into Russia.

Besides these two, who provided the expenses of the maps, printed "for the benefit of the Hellenes and Philhellenes," Rhiga mentions in his hymn:

> Sutzo, Moruzi, Pet, achi, Scanavis.
> Ghyka and Mavrogheni . . .

Inheritors of a Byzantine tradition, surrounded still by a faint Byzantine pomp, Greeks in education and sympathy, they were all glad to encourage any manifestations of cultured patriotism. They founded churches and supported schools with learned professors, like Eughenios Bulgaris, to whom Prince Alexander Mavrocordato addressed a versified credo; we have it in manuscript under the title:

> Ποίημα Ἀλεξάνδρου Μαυροκορδάτου πρώην ἡγεμόνος Μολ-
> δαβίας ἐρωτηθέντος παρὰ τοῦ σοφωτάτου Εὐγενίου τὶ
> πιστεύει.

Thus Rhiga happened to encounter a congenial and propitious atmosphere for his projects; not only in the Danubian Principalities. Austria-Hungary then seethed with nationalistic ferment.

At Budapest one could meet the fertile mind of George Zavira, whilst in Vienna the indefatigable brothers Pulliu were alike publishers and distributors of books, pamphlets and periodicals throughout the Levant; and they themselves edited a Greek newspaper, 'Εφημερίς.

In Vienna, too, G. Ventote brought out in 1790 a *Three Tongued Lexicon*; N. D. Darvari was preparing his *Introduction to the Greek Language*; a Macedonian, Basile Papa-Ephtemeou, looked forward to printing the translation of Goldsmith's *History of Hellas*.

All these cultivated men and a host of others received with great enthusiasm Rhiga's proposal to establish a secret society, simply termed Hetairia.

From all available sources we know to-day that his was not a narrow sort of nationalism. Infused by the spirit of the French Revolution, then in full swing, he aimed at the enlightenment of the Balkan peoples for securing freedom, each one, without infringing the freedom of others; nay, striving towards a mutual understanding. That is why Rhiga did not exclude the Turks from his society. In this direction he was a forerunner. But imperialist Austria of that time, which nourished designs on the Balkans, regarded Rhiga and his associates as dangerous rebels, and delivered them to the Belgrade executioners.

The shedding of their blood, however, was not in vain. In Shakespeare's words of King Lear to Cordelia:

There are some sacrifices on which the gods themselves throw incense.

Their death sent a frenzied stir through the Balkans and wherever there breathed a Greek soul. From Paris Koraes burst into fiery accents in his Σάλπισμα Πολεμιστήριον. The Vienna authorities had closed the publishing house of the brothers Pulliu, and their newspaper had ceased to exist; but a new one, with far greater influence, Λόγιος Ἑρμῆς, was to appear in its stead.

Greek writers everywhere, having tasted of Byron's warmly evocative poetry, spurred themselves to better achievements, backed by whole communities of rich merchants. That some called themselves Greeks and others Vlachs did not matter in the least. They were one in faith and one in admiration, amounting well nigh to a cult, for Hellenic culture.

And what books were theirs! To look at them nowadays

is to be proud of one's ancestors. The last pages give the names of the subscribers—people originating from so many different places, standing nevertheless here side by side in the joy of contributing, as lavishly as they could, to the accomplishment of an ideal which rose brilliantly before their eyes.

And while the Greek printing presses of Bucharest and Iassy worked incessantly, the Princes were sending many a young student to the newly opened school near Vatopedi, on Mount Athos, and to the Patriarchate school of Constantinople, the grants for such a purpose being embodied in beautifully ornamented charters.

A daughter of Prince Karadja, Ralou, gracious and conversant with Western literature, had the idea of likewise using the stage. She founded her own Greek theatre in Bucharest about the year 1818. It was lighted by tallow candles, that smoked and smelt dreadfully; but what did the audience care as long as they could hear on the stage the cadenced utterances of heroes who suffered and died for a noble cause?

As the theatre had patriotic aims in view, certain plays were especially chosen out of those that had just then a tremendous vogue in Paris through their revolutionary character, like Voltaire's *Death of Cæsar* and *Brutus* in the Greek translation of George Seruios. When the performance ended the streets of Bucharest resounded far into the night with Rhiga's Marseillaise and such declamatory verses in the mouth of Titus:

> *I am the son of Brutus, and in the depth of my heart*
> *It's liberty engraved . . .*

Some eighteen years later the same translation of *Brutus* came to be represented by the Athenian theatre of Athanases Skontzopoulou, in a Greece now liberated, master of herself, and ready to work out her own great future.

XI. THE ORACLE OF DODONA

HERODOTUS relates that from Ammon's Thebes two blackbirds took their flight, one towards Libya, the other over the region of Epirus, where it alighted on a tree and began to speak in a human manner. The people stood amazed at such a heavenly wonder, and paying heed to what it said, they raised close by that tree the Oracle of Dodona, which for long had attracted me, and now on my way to Jerusalem I passed to see it.

About sixty years ago the exact site of the Oracle was yet unknown. Travellers who fared along Epirus in search of Dodona had located it at various places, each one according to his own judgment. Questioned uncertain Byron:

> Oh ! where, Dodona, is thine aged grove,
> Prophetic fount, and oracle divine ?
> What valley echo'd the response of Jove ?
> What trace remaineth of the Thunderer's shrine ?

Now we are perfectly acquainted with it. At a distance of nearly two hours from Ianina, upon the way to Previsa, you reach the field of Tsaracoviste, shadowed by mountains, amongst which towers up the Tomarus, forest - covered in bygone days and alive with freshly running spring waters. It is a realm apart this. Perhaps the thought of an Oracle being once here increases the mysterious awe haunting around. You wait as if to hear strange forebodings in the air, and you realize why a temple was likewise dedicated to Zeus. Its votaries formed together a wise council who, judging and weighing circumstances, could utter illuminating indications on the future. They were aided by exterior signs of the divine presence: the rustle of the wind-stirred foliage; the clash against each other of hanging brazen discs; the flutter of doves on the wing.

Lured by the fame of the Oracle how many did not approach it with souls deeply thirsting for a mere word of solace ! It was Dodona that Crœsus the Lydian had asked for overcoming his hesitation, to wage or not a war on the Persians. To Dodona Ulysses made recourse to know if he was to return home openly or in a secret way. Dodona predicted the love with tragic ending of Io. Dodona's advice went to seek Jason before his venturing on the Argo. And Queen Olympias put her trust in Dodona with regard to the birth of Alexander.

Often the inquiries were inscribed on tiny slabs or rolls of lead, of which a good number were brought to light by the excavations; some referring to everyday, current matters of life. Thus, one wishes to be enlightened on the issue of his business enterprise; another craves for the dispelling of a suspicion about his wife's faith; a shepherd is anxious to find out how will they come out of the winter, he and his sheep.

What I should not give myself to get an answer to a question which is now incessantly burning in me ! But columns of the broken temple lie, scattered in the fields; and hushed for ever remains the Oracle.

XII. IANINA

I ARRIVED rather late, and dismounted at a hostel in
the market-place. Though tired, I could not close my
eyes. I felt an impatient, anticipatory pleasure at the
things I was going to see in Ianina, which I knew from hearsay
and from Greek folk-songs. The lake must have been quite
near, for a croaking of frogs became audible; it grew so intense
that it resounded through the whole town like a monster
concert.

Waking up in the morning and looking out of the window, I
caught sight of a mosque's minaret, deserted and pointless,
with a stork perched on the very top of it.

I encountered other such sights common in the Balkans
when I went out and walked along the streets to visit the
Greek gymnasium, of which the principal, Christos Souli,
happened to be a friend of mine. He emerged from the
library and showed me a manuscript of Byzantine music,
written by a certain Hieromonach Kallist in 1783; also a
Vienna printed book, *Nomothesia*, by Prince Karadgea, presented
to the school.

Then, accompanied by Christos Souli, I paid various calls.
One has to enter the houses, to mount wooden staircases with
carved balusters, to meet the welcome of courteous and fair
women, to sit on divans covered with soft, colourful, home-
woven rugs, and catch thus, as I did, a glimpse of the airy,
comfortable interiors in order to realize how polished and
soundly ordained life is here.

Notwithstanding the unrest and frequent disturbances, there
persisted throughout Epirus and Macedonia a tradition of
culture, enhanced by the close contact the people had always
kept with Constantinople and the Danubian Principalities on
one side and the West on the other.

We have cognisance of a high school in Ianina as far back
as the middle of the sixteenth century, because one of the
patriarchs at the time, Joasaph II, had studied in it. Another
school, that of Guma, attached to the monastery of the same
name, was opened in the year 1675.

This explains why Ianina has produced such a great number
of intellectuals, theologians, poets, painters and skilled artisans.
The patriarch Theolept I, at the outset of the sixteenth century,

was a native of Ianina, and so was Meletios, once Bishop of
Athens, author of a well-known *Ecclesiastical History*. From
Ianina likewise came Zotos Tsigaras, who attained to the
rank of Protospatharios, and was son-in-law to the Moldavian
Prince Peter the Lame. His tomb can still be seen at St.
George's Church of the Greeks in Venice, under an inscribed
black marble stone placed there by his brother Apostol. Both
he and Zotos Tsigaras proved great benefactors and helpers
to the printing of Greek books.

In a recently discovered Greek gospel at Cairo, which
displays a carpet-like variety of ornamentation, the colophon
reads:

" This godly and sacred gospel has been written by Hieromonach Anthim of Ianina in 1640."

Another illuminated gospel I found at the Metropolitan
Church in Ianina is due to Bishop Matthew, an illustrious
calligrapher. It has golden initials, and the frontispieces show
interlaced branches with flowers, amongst which saintly
apparitions move about freely, enlivened by a fresh breath of
the Renaissance. In this aspect it differs from the two other
gospels of his at the Treasury of the Holy Sepulchre, but in
all he proudly notes and is anxious for one to know that he
comes " from Pogoniani of old Epirus "—

Πωγωνιανῆς ἐκ Παλαιᾶς Ἠπείρου.

It was by chance that at one of the antique shops I came
upon a bronze-beaten disc with fantastic animals and a remarkable silver plaque of a ' Deesis,' that is, our Lord enthroned,
with the Virgin Mary on His right and St. John the Baptist
on the left, bearing an inscription to the effect that it was made
" at the expense of the Ianina Brasiers' Guild "—

Δαπάνη τοῦ Ρουφετίου τῶν Χαλκιάδων τοῦ Ἰωαννίνου.

With a heartfelt throb I read the line, reflecting on the
important rôle of the guilds and the precious heritage they had
bequeathed us, especially the silversmiths. Who ever saw their
exquisitely wrought objects in filigree and did not consider
them equal to the best of Damascus ?

And how could this honest, painstaking work, expressive of
an individuality, stand the competition of the cheap, artistically indifferent products, made into numberless copies by a
greedy foreign market ? Nothing but remnants of the guilds
cling to the bazaar of Ianina. I passed them whilst going to the
right-hand side of the lake, where the town extends into a

quarter dominated by the palace and mosque that once belonged to the notorious Ali Pasha.

One might have regarded him as a romantic figure were it not for his cruelty and his destructive bent. To dust he brought whole villages in the flower of their development. Yet, unwillingly, he did one good, for it was on his account that representatives of England and France, William Martin Leake and Pouqueville respectively, were sent to Ianina.

Both of them being writers, their books left us a great deal of information. And, as the time of Ali Pasha corresponded with the awakened interest for classicism, some English travellers reached Greece by way of Ianina, among them Lord Byron. To his verses in *Don Juan*:

> *He leads them through the hall, and without stopping,*
> *On through a farther range of goodly rooms,*
> *Splendid but silent, save in one, where dropping,*
> *A marble fountain echoes through the glooms*
> *Of night . . .*

he added the note: " I recollect being received by Ali Pasha in a room containing a marble basin and fountain."

And in a letter to his mother, dated Previsa, November 12, 1809:

" Ali Pasha said he was certain I was a man of birth, because I had small ears, curling hair and little, white hands, and expressed himself pleased with my appearance and garb. He told me to consider him as a father whilst I was in Turkey, and said he looked on me as his son. Indeed, he treated me like a child, sending me almonds and sugared sherbet, fruit and sweetmeats twenty times a day." On his entering Ianina:

> *Amidst no common pomp the despot sate,*
> *While busy preparations shook the court,*
> *Slaves, eunuchs, soldiers, guests and santons wait;*
> *Within a palace, and without, a fort:*
> *Here men of every clime appear to make resort.*

Scarcely one hundred and twenty-five years have elapsed since Byron wrote the above in *Childe Harold's Pilgrimage*, and what a change to-day ! Where is the bustle, and where the clatter of arms, and the plots and the intrigues ? Gone. All swept away by the unsparing wind of time. The warm sun around seems to vibrate with the unceasing monotonous murmur of insects. It somewhat increases the sense of loneliness, which, save for the stir in the fishermen's cottages, pervades

the entire island of the lake. Seldom do people tread its
paths. Here only churches and churches, low, humble,
trying, as it were, to hide themselves under the trees. But
when you get inside them what a richness of ecclesiastical art !

A thing of beauty is a joy for ever. . . .

And many an afternoon I took delight in looking at what was
most pleasingly rare among the icons, the altar crosses, the
silver lamps, the heavy pieces of embroidery, the chalices, the
caskets and reliquaries encrusted with stones in sparkling hues.
What a pity, I said to myself, that when a group of Byzantine
scholars in Athens, such as Nicou Bees, Amantos, Sotiriou,
began to study these works, mostly by native artists, the war
broke out and interrupted—interrupted, let us hope, and not
stopped for good—their valuable researches.

I BEGAN my researches with Zagori. From town to town I went, and seeing everywhere large stone houses utterly deserted, I realized the deep pathos of many a folk-song, trembling with tears and longing. For a time now adverse circumstances induced people to go and seek a living abroad. One of the songs begins:

Κίνησαν τὰ καράβια τὰ Ζαγοριανά,
Κίνησεν κι' ὁ καλός μου, πάει 'σ τὴν ξενιτειά. . . .

Started on the vessels, the vessels of Zagori,
Started too my dear one, he's gone to foreign lands.

Another song makes the Danube resound with the voices of those who sail upon it, and heard above them all is one bidding his beloved to wed somebody else, for he will never, never return again.

Not a few of the expatriated, having attained high social rank, from a noble ambition and piety, used to endow or build churches at their birthplaces, as prosperous English merchants did in the city of London. According to Byzantine usage, such benefactors were pictorially represented on the church walls.

At St. Elias of Zitza I was greatly interested in a wooden cross, minutely carved, dated 1776, the gift of Wallachia's Metropolitan Dositheus Filittis from Pogoniani, who bequeathed it as a legacy, remembering that he went first to school at this monastery, as likewise the Patriarch Jeremiah had done about two hundred and fifty years before. At an early date the particular Zitza site was considered worthy of being consecrated by a monastery. And now, standing on its height and spanning the view as far as the eyes could reach towards the shimmering horizon, I gave full credit to Byron for his description in *Childe Harold*:

Monastic Zitza ! From thy shady brow,
Thou small, but favour'd spot of holy ground !
Where'er we gaze, around, above, below,
What rainbow tints, what magic charms are found ! . . .

How numerous the elect shades that haunt the quiet streets of Pogoniani ! It was one of them, Pano Pepanas, who, as a

rich Epirot merchant of Venice, brought out at his own expense
in 1672 the versified Chronicle of Stavrinos Vestiarius, an
Epirot also, in his own words:

Μαλσιανὴ ἡ χώρα του καὶ Δελβίνου μερίδα.

Passing through Monodendron, I inquired and found out the
house, abandoned wholly to desolation, of the Mishou family.
One of its members, a lawyer by profession, is now living in
Ianina.

On my descent from Zagori I tarried a little at the Moliv-
doskepasti, so named from its roof in lead, which does not
exist any longer, and empty altogether is the monastery inside,
stripped of its contents. Only the white skeleton of walls
remain, with widely yawning windows, like a galley made
useless and cast ashore by storm. In its actual state, however,
it serves to emphasize tersely the faith of bygone days, when an
emperor of Byzantium, Andronicus Comnenus, used to have
the monastery under his own devout care.

Up on the left, commanding the plain of Velas, stands the
Sosianou Monastery, dedicated to the Annunciation, and built
by G. Simota and his wife Theodora, whose lot it was to live
and die in Moldavia, far away from their Epirot home.

Even higher, on a mountainous ridge more suitable for an
eagle's nest, the Vlasiou Monastery raises itself solitarily.
A fresco of its interior wall shows two full-sized figures holding
between them a miniature church. Both wear red tunics and
fur cap of the same colour. The Greek inscription says:
" Kir Constantin, humble founder of this church, and his son,
Kir George."

I learned that a grant had been bestowed by Prince Nicholas
Mavrocordato on the Greek school of Coritza. The bishop of
that city, Eudokios Kurila, whom I knew from Mount Athos,
gave me the year of the deed (1728), adding that it had come
about through the intermission of Joasaph, Patriarch of
Ochrida.

A remarkable personality this, originating from Moschopoli,
whither I now proceed, and I do it with the eager sentiment of a
pilgrim. For Moschopoli reached a high degree of culture
previous to being sacked by the wild bands of Ali Pasha. Its
achievements were extolled in songs and legends. It possessed
a printing house, the second established in Turkey after that
of Constantinople, and a superior school under the name of
'Ακαδημία with professors like Theodore Cavalioti, author
of many works, whom Sathas calls γραμματικὸς ἄριστος.

Another learned man, Daniel the Jeromonach, wrote a Λεξικὸν Τετράγλωσσον reprinted by William Martin Leake in his *Researches*.

A few hamlets and shrines still remain in Moschopoli, amongst which the best preserved is that of St. Nicholas, erected by a certain Archon Vretou in 1721. I noticed inside a silver cross; though simple, in filigree with a carnelion, it has a special value, for tradition says it belonged to the Patriarch Joasaph.

With a sorrowful heart I advanced through the debris and halted for a while in what was the core of the city, and where the fountain goes on with its flow, adding to the acute sense of desolation.

Opposite, on the shady height, lies the Monastery of St. John the Baptist. An inscription in Greek over the church door reads as follows: " This godly and sacred church was erected through the help and expense of the most noble and esteemed Archon George Gutzo in the year 1632." I looked into three manuscript codices of the monastery, photographing some of the pages; they are all-important for the light they throw on Moschopoli and its emigrants, who later formed such strong colonies in Vienna and Budapest.

Through roundabout roads I reached Arghirocastro, which extends upon the hills and is guarded by a silver-white tower that gives it the name. To walk the streets here and be faced now and again with beautiful distant vistas, to be caught in the weird silence enwrapping the fortress-like Turkish houses, is to enjoy new, unexpected impressions.

In a central quarter I found the Greek metropolis, whose church occupies the site of a temple, for a number of gargoyles and inscribed marbles are built in its walls. Conversing with Bishop Pantelimon, I drew his attention to three endowment charters concerning the Drianou Monastery of his diocese.

" I have a suspicion," I said, " that the authors of these charters, the Princes Ghykas and Lupu, hailed from Epirus."

" I can say nothing, unless there is any mention in our old codex."

We turned the heavy leaves to the events related at the beginning of the sixteenth century, and we read:

" About this time the inhabitants of Zervati and other Epirot cities, on account of incessant oppression and disturbances, dispersed towards Wallachia. . . ."

" A better proof we cannot have," I remarked.

Then, in the company of two monks, I went a short distance by car; thence three whole hours of ascent on foot through a rough gorge, until there appeared, on the hill-top, Drianou, looking more like a farmhouse than a monastery. Only a herdsman kept watch on it. The cloisters were changed into stables, and the church left to itself,

With no priest or deacon,

as the song has it. But one gets a finely carved iconostas, and in the ancient diptych, containing the names of benefactors for whom prayers were offered, one encounters some of princes, kings and Byzantine emperors.

When I departed Drianou was dimly contoured on the skies, and there lurked invisible the spectre of decay. Not so long from now one will hardly know that a holy shrine had ever existed here by the name of Drianou. My thoughts became sadder as dusk grew; whilst from all sides fireflies began to glow, multitudes of them, innumerable, fading here and springing there in a vivid, continuous glitter of sparks. They reminded me of a passage closing the pages of *Præterita*, in which Ruskin speaks of the fireflics hc once saw in the vicinity of Siena. From his descriptive manner, from the nostalgic repetition of " How they shone, how they shone !" one gets the impression that the fireflies were nothing but dreams, dreams, illumining our poor, dark, and transient passage upon earth.

XIV. THE MONASTERIES OF METEORA

WHEN I saw Calabaka with its houses, and people moving about under the shadow of the giant rocks of Meteora, Gulliver's Lilliput came to my mind; and as I gazed more closely at the rocks, sheer and steep, rising to great heights, where monasteries stood perched upon their summits, I thought to myself, How and by what means did the first monks get up there?

Nothing but a strong and overpowering faith could supply the explanation, and it was faith indeed that urged Saint Athanasius to set out from Mount Athos and find his anchorite way to a cave on the outskirts of Calabaka. Then one day, by God's will, he ascended the mightiest rock of Meteora and laid the foundation of the first shrine dedicated to the Transfiguration.

Here, two years before his earthly end in 1381, the blessed Joasaph joined him. A princely scion this, by lay name John Uroš, son of King Simeon. His sister, who used to sign herself Maria Anghelini Duca Paleologou, was the wife of Thomas Preliubovič, Despot of Ianina.

Such high and rich connections brought an advantage to the newly erected monastery in the shape of endowments and gifts lavishly bestowed. Soon its fame spread through the length and breadth of the country, so much so that it drew hither two brethren belonging to the noble Apsara family of Ianina, Nectarius and Theophanes, who ventured to build a second monastery—St. Barlaam. In their tracks followed others, until no less than fourteen peaks of Meteora came to be covered with sacred shrines.

From the very start the singular position of these monasteries accounted for their often entering into the folk productions. Such, for instance, that widely diffused song:

’Εσεῖς πουλιὰ τοῦ Γρεβενοῦ, κι’ ἀηδόνια τοῦ Μετσόβου,
’Εσεῖς καλὰ τὸν ξέρετε αὐτὸν τὸν παπᾶ Θύμιο. . . .

> *You birds of Grevena, Metzovu's nightingales*
> *Full well you know, you heard of Father Thymio.*

And the poem goes on to relate how he, Father Thymio,

> *Broke in all the forts and all the monasteries,*
> *Except for Barlaam, he could never tread on;*
> *For up it stood on marble, and up on high cliffs. . . .*

The easiest monastery to approach from Calabaka is that of
St. Stephen. You climb the mountain until you are level
with the monastery, and then you cross over, through a little
drawbridge thrown over the chasm. At one side of the court
you walk towards the church. It has a long narthex supported
by six stone columns; while inside, the iconostas strikes you
more than anything else. It is a remarkable piece of wooden
sculpture. As I look at it in the trembling rays of the tapers,
the little birds seem to take wing from amongst the intertwined
leaves and flowers, so masterfully is it all carved.

" This beautiful work," says the Abbot, " and every object
you see here, the icons, the precious hangings, the holy vessels,
the lamps, constitute old devotional offerings. Those were the
times when Greek Eastern Orthodoxy shone throughout the
Balkans, irrespective of race and frontier. I will show you
some relics that came from beyond the Danube."

He carefully displayed two caskets in ornamented silver
filigree, one containing the head of St. Haralambos, the other
a finger of St. John the Baptist, over which gleamed the miniature portraits of the donors, Vladislav and Princess Neaxa,
dated 1488. Being both credited with miraculous healing
virtues, how deeply were they once revered ! Of what solace
they proved to many a depressed heart ! I had under my eyes
letters from sick people, full of tears, beseeching that one or
other of the shrines should be sent to them as the last hope of
their prevailing over death.

I afterwards passed to the monastery of the Transfiguration.
For some time the monks here had cut out a staircase from the
rock leading to the monastery. But I preferred their more
primitive device of the rope, worked by a windlass, a net being
attached to its end. This I stretched on the ground, got in,
and up I went, swinging into the air, with my head out of the
net. For one moment, as I gazed below under me, I shivered;
dark and profound yawned the precipice. Suppose, I thought,
the monks pulling the rope got tired and let it loose. Suppose
the rope does not hold any more—have not I heard it said they
do not change the rope until after it breaks ? No sooner,
however, had I entertained such fears than I found myself
hoisted on to the platform of the monastery, where the Abbot,
short in stature, with his face almost covered by a black beard,
waited for me. Unexpectedly he began to chuckle.

" Is anything the matter ?" I inquired.

" Please," he said, " don't think I am laughing at you. A
story has just crossed my mind; why shouldn't I tell you ?

Not long ago Queen Mary of Rumania paid a visit to us. Keen as she was on Byzantine art, and as women are not allowed up here, I arranged that some of our best treasures should be taken down to her.

" Meanwhile, I do not know how it happened, the Queen saw the net hanging from the rope, jumped in it, made a sign, and, would you believe it ?   There she appeared, facing me in the monastery.   I looked around astounded, and not a little annoyed.   Of course, I asked her to leave immediately.   ' It's unlawful,' I remonstrated.   ' No woman ever set foot inside the monastery, not even any of the Byzantine Empresses.'

" The Queen, not understanding my Greek, turned to her attendant interpreter.   He explained, whereupon the Queen stooped and, with outstretched arms on my shoulders, kissed me on the forehead.   ' Peculiar thing,' I said to myself; ' I protest, and she embraces me !'   Afterwards I understood. The Queen's interpreter had been afraid to repeat my words, and had said: ' Oh, your Majesty, the Reverend Father says how very happy he is to see you here.' "

After we had had a good laugh together I accompanied the Abbot to his cell.   From a mysteriously hidden cupboard he brought out a Greek codex bearing this inscription in red letters:

" It was written the present book in the most kingly monastery of the Meteora, in the year 1570."

Copied from a far older original, it related the life story of St. Athanasius and, implicitly, the commencement of the monastery of the Transfiguration.   This codex has been thoroughly studied and published by Nicou Bees in Βυζαντίς, of 1909.   The same author has carried out a learned and painstaking research in the libraries of Meteora, and has given us a catalogue of their books.

One would have never guessed how many rare and valuable printed works and scripts were gathered in such an out-of-the-way, secluded abode of the monks.   For security's sake they have in recent years all been transferred to the National Library of Athens.   There one can now see the two Gospel manuscripts in parchment of the eleventh century, which, to his regret, Robert Curzon was unable to remove from the monastery of the Transfiguration despite the many pieces of gold he offered.   They deserve great admiration, and in his *Visits to the Monasteries in the Levant* he wrote, remembering their pages illuminated with cypress-trees and peacocks and arabesques: " Such books as these would be treasured in the finest national collection in Europe."

Another Gospel manuscript, formerly in the possession of St. Barlaam, has to be noted, because it makes mention of its painter, Andrew, who

Various figures craftily depicted.

καλλιεργήσαντα χροαῖς ποικίλαις.

His was the style used previous to the fourteenth century, when the Byzantine art assumed a new aspect, more vivid and free, brought about by the so-called Cretan and Macedonian schools. We have excellent specimens of them both at St. Barlaam and the Transfiguration, due to representative masters, such as Frangos Catellanos of Thebes and Theophanes the Cretan. Painters of the same schools are later responsible for the work done at other Meteora monasteries, such as St. Ypapanti and Holy Trinity, where on the narthex of its church one can read the lines:

" It has been painted by Demetrius Zuki of Calarites and his pupil George. 1784."

On my return to Calabaka I tarried one evening at St. Stephen. Whoever has caught a view of the Thessalian fields from here and has not conjured it up afterwards in his dreams ? The sun had set, and in the mellow, soft glow it left behind Mount Pindus grew loftier. The horizon seemed to melt away in the purple-tinted distance, and there between, heavy with memories of golden days, the river Peneus passed on to the Tempean legendary haunts. All these not only, as Walter de la Mare would say:

Beauty took from those who loved them
In other days,

but their beauty is further enhanced and transfigured by some divinely inspired literature. There, imbued by an ever-enduring breath, gods, goddesses and nymphs move, created by a pagan faith now dead for centuries, and replaced by another Christian one, which in its turn appeared to be quite on the wane.

For behold ! Out of fourteen monasteries, no more than four remained, forlorn and impoverished, scarcely inhabited by three or four inmates. It is not far from the time when these too will disappear, and the generations to come will only know about the Meteora monasteries from books of wayfarers or from writers like myself, at once belated pilgrims and devotees of a pious tradition.

XV. WALKS IN ATHENS

ONE morning I heard the telephone bell ringing in the hotel room where I was lodging in Athens.

"Hallo, hallo. . . ." I was startled. At the other end a feigned voice burst into laughter.

"Who is speaking?"

"Guess!" came the answer.

"Well, is it you, Anita? When did you arrive? Why didn't you inform me?"

"I wanted to surprise you."

"And where are you now?"

"Here, in the hotel. I'm coming at once. . . ."

When she appeared on the threshold of my door I drew her by the hand and threw the windows wide open. "Behold!" I said.

"Heavens! The Acropolis!" Anita exclaimed.

Straight ahead under the sunrise the crimsoned columns, framing the distant blue, seemed, as it were, to detach themselves and float together like a fairy palace of wonder.

"How long I have yearned to see it! And my dream is so unexpectedly fulfilled that I can hardly trust my eyes. May it not be a vanishing illusion?"

"No, no, my dear. All is real, the Acropolis and we two here beyond any fears. But we mustn't lose time; let us hurry out."

We strolled in the park under the verdant foliage. At every step Anita turned her head in amazement.

"Oh, the palm-trees. . . . How tall! And those bushes with white flowers, what are they?"

"Myrtles, sung by the poets."

"Really? I didn't know . . ."

"That is the advantage of a journey to Greece, you meet with what you have so often read about. Here is the acanthus serving as a motive of decoration for monuments, and the laurel, sacred to Apollo, that crowned the heroes. Don't you feel its bitter perfume?"

"Yes, I do. But the whole air seems to be fragrant."

"So it is, owing to the sun; even the weeds here give out an aroma when crushed between the fingers."

At the Zappeion we stopped.

BRONZE DISC, WORK OF IANINA

WOOD CROSS, MOUNT ATHOS

CARVED WOOD AMBON,
ST. GEORGE'S CHURCH, ZAGORÀ

(*Facing p.* 60)

HOLY TRINITY MONASTERY, WITH A VIEW OF MOUNT PINDUS AND
THE PENEOUS

VIEW OF MOUNT SINAI MONASTERY

(*Facing p.* 61)

" Look now," I said. " Few places in the world can speak more to the imagination. Entire historical periods unfold themselves under one's eyes. On the left, Pentelic's marbled heights; in front, the Saronic deep blue; then near here the temple of Olympian Zeus, I mean that solitary group of columns by Hadrian's Gate; and up on the right, the ever-guarding Acropolis.

" Do you notice ? In proportion as the sun mounts and the shadows increase, it grows in magnificence. It isn't only the skill of a refined simplicity, but its renown stands consecrated in writing by countless wayfarers. And what celebrated names amongst them ! The impetuous Byron, the solemn Chateaubriand, the doubting Renan, who was compelled to change his song of praise into a humble and fervid prayer. Now it's our turn to get a closer view of it."

" Let's walk, shall we ? I've always thought that the best way to the Acropolis would be to go on foot, like a pilgrim."

" I agree. We think alike. It really is the best way."

Arrived at the end of the ascending road, we drew aside and tarried a while before the theatre of Dionysus.

" Under the Parthenon," I explained, " fittingly hewn out in the hill slope as other theatres of yore. But when you sit thinking that this is the oldest, the beginner of the Greek tragedy ! In its early phase the whole performance ministered to a ritualistic aim. With recitals, songs and dances one cele-brated the triumph of nature, symbolized in the death and resurrection of Dionysus, whose parts came to be gradually taken by the Homeric heroes. Passing to the Propylæa, I should add, it was likewise a religious procession that mounted the sacred steps. You would realize things better at the entrance of the Erechtheium."

" Do you see the olive-tree over there ? It is on the spot of a most ancient one, personifying the very lot of the city. The Persians burned it once, but it sprang up again. A branch of that olive-tree, embellished with ribbons, used to be carried about by the fairest among maidens, purposely chosen; such a queen of the procession being at later days superseded by a wooden statue of the goddess, for whom the Athenian virgins prepared a beautifully precious robe. . . ."

Inquired Anita:

" How do we know these things ?"

" We find them all in the frieze of the Parthenon, which is but a marble transmutation of the Panathenaic festival."

Soon after we descended the hill and slowly took the road to

Piræus.   At a little distance I showed Anita the brook running
between empty shores:

" The Ilissus !"

" This is it ?"

" Do not be astonished, for it must once have been different.
Plato speaks of green and shaded freshness.   Here, somewhere,
he brought together Socrates and Phædrus to debate those
daringly matchless speculations on love and immortality.

Previous to being embodied, the soul enjoyed an ever-bright
celestial region, the memory of which is temporarily lost.
But, if it happens to encounter on the way a certain beauty,
then suddenly the soul appears bewildered, catching a dream-
like, far-away glimpse of the undying vision it had known before;
and it would much desire to soar aloft, seized by rapture, by
a feverish unrest akin to madness.

And the particular being that occasioned it finds herself in
great adoration, for she is the expression of divine beauty upon
earth, she it is who weaves the dream-bridge of the soul's ascent
to heavens.   Do you understand ?"

Anita nodded and gazed straight at me.

" I should say, yes, dear professor; but you don't speak in
a cold manner.   Something stirs you."

" Socrates was not quite himself either under the spell of
the nymphs around him."

We proceeded to the National Museum, and, starting with
the discoveries at Mycenæ, I said: " A whole treasure, unknown
up to not long ago, which unveils the old Ægean achievement
in relation to that of Phœnicia and Crete.   What richness, and
what artistically wrought things !   Here are masks of beaten
gold to mould faces gone into dust, and here breastplates, and
thin discs variedly designed, and banqueting cups, and butter-
flies for adornment, and finger rings, all in gold; and in gold,
too, many strange miniatures of goddesses, of crowns, of
altars—a profusion of gold scattered in the graves.

Certain objects correspond to the description of Homer, who
related a great deal about the Mycenæan heroes; and, from
Homer, Schliemann proceeded to bring into the light of day
what was left by Homer in the realm of song.   But we had
better pass to the undisturbed serenity of the hall of sculpture."

Anita gazed on all sides and spoke:

" Where should one stop first ?   They vie with each other
in mastery of craftsmanship."

" Because these artists gave us archetypes that float above the
centuries.   They stood in the company of gods, seeing the

world through a high Olympian standard, and so they caught in marble what Plato did in his wide, embracing mind. There is Tegea's head, and Ariadne, and the nimble body of the Dancer, her raiment waving to the rhythm of the steps—ideal beauties all, towards whom tend our aspirations.

"And the bas-relief from Eleusis! Two goddesses, having between them the favourite youth to be initiated. They spin in one's memory the golden myth of the rape of Persephone. Further on, the funerary stelæ, which represent little familiar scenes; but, examined attentively, what significance they take on! Look especially at the one of Hegiso. The maid, handing her the jewel casket, is sad; sadder still the mistress who stretches out her hand to the ornaments of earthly pleasure. In her eyes, in her gesture, in the entire expression of her delicate face she seems to say: 'I don't use them any more; I don't enjoy them. I enjoy nothing now, for I sleep here in a cold grave, and sleep I shall to-morrow and after to-morrow and always the unending sleep of extinction.'"

My voice must have sounded queer, for Anita turned at once, and taking me by the hand:

"Let's get out in the air and go to Phaleron."

We sat at a café on the seashore. In the calm of approaching night only the voice of oyster-sellers with loaded baskets was heard crying out. A slightly scented breeze breathed from the waters at large, tinged afar by the setting sun towards Cithæron, whilst on the other side the golden beams moved still on the summits of Hymethus.

"In such an evening," I began.

"Please," interrupted Anita, "don't tell me anything. In silence, with no thoughts whatever, let us absorb in our souls these priceless moments. After many years, when elsewhere, we shall recall them from the past: 'Do you remember Phaleron, that evening? . . .'"

XVI. TO THE ISLAND OF RHODES

"FROM Athens," I asked Anita, "where shall we go?"

"Haven't you got any plan?"

"I would suggest Rhodes. Apart from the pleasure of visiting the island, you will be able to seek your paternal house. Your father hailed from Rhodes, didn't he?"

"Yes, but he left the island so long ago, and he has since sold the house."

"Nevertheless, wouldn't you like to see it with your own eyes?"

"Of course I should, and it is very kind of you to have thought of it."

Embarking at Piræus and proceeding for a while, I spoke to Anita:

"Do you know how they call our boat? Kalithea. It is the name of a well in Rhodes and of its guardian nymph."

"Oh, to travel on such a boat and on a sea like this!"

Anita pointed to the waters. Deep blue and very calm they stretched out; on the surface only tiny ripples stirred ceaselessly shining in the sunlight. Time flew quickly. At dawn, after a short night, little islands began to appear, forerunners of the one we soon greeted loudly: "Rhodes, Rhodes!" It rose from the sea; first the grey city walls, then over them, behind, the roofs, towers and minarets, interlaced with tall cypresses reaching the sky.

As soon as anchor was cast, we hurried out on a road along the walls. The transparent air seemed to throb with perfumes —especially that of roses in great profusion, white, red and yellow roses. The island bore its flower name worthily. Gardens embellished the bay, and villas and numerous windmills, but all dumb, with no wheels, serving as dwelling-houses.

"This is a new part of the town," I said. "If we are to look for the house, we must go inside the walls."

The Turkish domination had left an influence on the narrow streets which ran, as it were, leisurely, aimless. The facing upper floors of the buildings inclined towards each other; being connected here and there by stone arches and by fresh, growing, leaf-canopies. Under the shade of a plane-tree we saw nicely arranged tables and stools of a café, and we sat down. When the Greek owner of the place came to us, I ventured:

"Listen, friend, there was in Rhodes a rich family by the name of Dandrea. Do you happen to know the whereabouts of their house?"

"Sorry," he answered, "I am not from this island; but I shall fetch someone who knows everything here."

We did not wait long. An old man, short and slim, approached gently and gave his name, "Kosta Lugadi, warden of the Metropolitan church."

"We are strangers," I began. . . .

"Good health to you both," interrupted Kosta Lugadi, "and welcome!"

I felt bound to respond with thanks and then I continued:

"We want to find out the house that belonged to this young lady's father, a native of Rhodes. Have you heard of one Dandrea, Apostol Dandrea?"

"Have I heard of him, of Apostol Dandrea. . . . Why, we were friends. And you say this is his daughter and he is alive?"

Turning to Anita: "Remember me to him. . . . Eh, scarcely was Dandrea eighteen, when he wandered into foreign lands. And in ten years' time he came back. I see him still, young and proud of himself, entering the church on Sunday. A whisper passed from man to man: 'It is Apostol Dandrea!' And when they sprinkled him with rose-water, six gold pieces he put in the collection disc so that all were both astonished and pleased. He did not stay long, about three weeks; then he went and has never returned since."

Kosta Lugadi paused with a heavy sigh, adding: "Now I'll show you the house."

We walked a few minutes to a crossing, where Kosta Lugadi stopped: "Here it is, at the corner, with a balcony on the Street of the Knights."

Anita's eyes filled with tears. "My poor father, when I'll tell him. . . . For some years, burdened by old age, his mind often wanders back here. I don't know how and whence he got hold of a photograph. He takes it out and calls me: 'Look, my dear, where I was born; the house of my parents I left behind and I shall never see again.'

"I recognize it now. . . . A fountain there, under two plane-trees and the mosque nearby. Father spoke also of a certain church overlooking our garden."

"Yes, the Chapel of St. Mark. It is concealed by a wall

5

recently erected, you can hardly catch a glimpse of its Byzantine dome."

Before taking leave, most courteously did Kosta Lugadi direct us down the Street of the Knights. On either side there rose Gothic palaces, blackened by time. Over their gates in carved wood one distinguished bas-reliefs, dates, heraldic figures; whilst dragon-shaped gargoyles watched from the eaves. We passed in turn the Hospice of France, the Hospice of Provence and that of Aragon with a bridge thrown on the street and yet another—still in use to the present day. Anita stood enraptured at its entrance, exclaiming: " What a delightful spot !" From the dusky depths of the court there came into sight a marble well, ornamented with lattice-iron. Close to it stairs of stone ascended towards the light of the first store, whence creeping vine and wistaria hung in long, silky festoons over the marble well and the stairs of stone. Here the Grand Master comes to reside during three months of the year amid portraits, maps and flags of the various nations forming the Order of St. John, whom the faith for a common goal succeeded in keeping united in life and death.

" And how long did the Knights Hospitallers rule the Island of Rhodes ?"

" About two centuries; but what are two centuries against the background of a whole Hellenic past ? Some of its artistic remains are gathered in a museum of this very Street of the Knights. Let us go in."

Everything one gazes upon possesses undoubted value. Here is Aphrodite, called *Pudica*, as a piece of veil still clings on the goddess's hips. There another statue of Aphrodite. With both hands she draws aside her abundant waving locks in order to free the eyes, which, half-opened, suggest that she is desirous not to see but rather to be seen in the full whiteness of her body, fallen on one knee. And alone in a room, receiving the light from one side, there is a mortuary stele that bears the Greek names of Crito and Timaritza. It represents a mother stretching her hand round the neck of her daughter with bent head. The tenderness of the expression inclines one to ask: Who were they ? What joy, if any, was theirs in life ? The more so captivating is the enigmatic artistry. I am tempted to whisper what Keats did to his Grecian Urn:

> *Thou, silent form, dost tease us out of thought*
> *As doth eternity. . . .*

The museum extends into a garden. Two cypresses frame

slabs of mosaics. Oleander flowers add to a luxurious wealth of interlaced greenery. Inscribed marbles sparkle in the sun. My thoughts fly to Laocoon. I tell Anita:

" I should like to see Laocoon here, not the original, which is to be found at the Vatican, but a good copy of it."

" Why just the Laocoon ?"

" Because it is the creation of Rhodes. Its contemplation would give an insight into the great development of the Island, which alone could explain the production of such work, a triumph of pondered expression in art. Indeed, there once existed in Rhodes a famous Rhetorical School, where men like Cicero and Julius Cæsar came to study. Ranking high among the poets was Apollonius the Rhodian, author of *Argonautica*. In the stormy passion of Jason and Medea he successfully touched the chords of a deep romantic love that was to attain later the hauntingly intense emotion of Virgil's Dido and Æneas. Then we have Posidonius who, resuming in himself all the richness of Hellenic philosophy, infused it with a breath of Eastern mysticism, preparing thus in a sense the way of Christianity."

XVII. DAPHNE

AS I left Antioch on my way to Daphne I fell to thinking of a story in Greek by Deacon James, *The Life of St. Pelagia.* It relates at the beginning how a group of prelates assembled in Antioch under the head of Nonnus, Bishop of Edessa. Whilst they were conversing at the doorway of a basilica, lo! suddenly there appeared, riding on an ass, Pelagia, first amongst the Antiochian actresses.

Ivory-white she gleamed, naked in body, under a thin robe of gauze ornamented with gold and brilliant stones. Her full, seductive lips bestowed frequent smiles on the young men who followed her in a splendid train. When she passed by a subtle and disturbing fragrance filled the air behind her. The prelates turned away their heads as from a great sin.

Only the blessed Nonnus gazed intently at her, and did not remove his eyes until she went out of his view. Then, turning to the prelates, he said:

" Did not the sight of her beauty delight you ?"

They all kept silent. Once more he asked:

" Did not the sight of her beauty delight you ?" And, as they again answered him nothing, the blessed Nonnus added: " In truth it delighted me exceedingly, and well content was I with her beauty."

One catches here a glimpse of Christianity striving hard to free itself from the overwhelmingly voluptuous pagan atmosphere in which Antioch lay enwrapt. Its inhabitants prided themselves on being Hellenes. The founder of the city, Seleucus Nicator, descended from the gods. His mother, Laodice, had pleased Apollo much when he saw her in distant Macedonia. He left her as a token of love a ring engraved with an anchor, and it was with the mark of an anchor in his thigh that Seleucus Nicator, offspring of such union, happened to come into the world.

Bearing this in mind, one could understand why the Seleucids, who boasted of their dynasty's divine origin, were ambitiously eager to rear a new kind of Delphi in the vicinity of Antioch. They built a sacred road, bordered on either side with sumptuous pavilions, statues, colonnades, a Castalia fountain, leading up to the grove of Daphne and the rich, oracular spring.

Among others, Hadrian obtained from it, whilst yet doubtful about the future, a presage of his elevation to the Roman throne; whereupon he tried to choke up the spring in order to prevent it making any further prophecies. But, in spite of his selfish whim, the water went on flowing, as it still does, from the stony mountain, and falls in tumultuous streams, in sheets of silver and in clouds of foam.

Above them shining creepers quiver and ancient oaks grow, intermingled with mulberry-trees, with poplars and with willows, giving the place of honour to the oleanders, enormous flaming clusters such as I had also seen at Delphi.

How indifferent nature is to the works of man! Exuberant it continues to grow, whereas in vain I seek after a sign, a mere trace of the shrines and monuments once adorning the haunts of Daphne. It weighs heavy upon me, this plunging into the abyss of a whole past.

Yet, no less than in 362 A.D. the temple of Apollo still existed. We know it from Julian the Apostate. On his expedition to Persia he came here. It was a festival day. And at first the fact struck him ominously that the portal did not hang, as customary, with green branches of laurel. Inside the temple he encountered an utter desolation. The altar seemed cold, no offerings, no scented smoke of myrrh and incense; and, as if to heighten the sense of irony, an old priest entered with a goose under his arm. For lack of others, he had brought himself something to the sacrifice.

Not long before Julian sent out a representative to consult the Oracle of Delphi. And it gave answer in a voice that was to be silenced for ever, this last swan-lament being couched in obsessingly melodious cadences:

εἴπατε τῷ βασιλῆϊ, χαμαὶ πέσε δαίδαλος αὐλα·
οὐκέτι Φοῖβος ἔχει καλύβαν, οὐ μάντιδα δάφνην,
οὐ παγὰν λαλέουσαν· ἀπέσβετο καὶ λάλον ὕδωρ.

In Swinburne's translation:

Tell the king, on earth has fallen the glorious dwelling,
*   And the watersprings that spake are quenched and dead.*
Not a cell is left the God, no roof, no cover;
*   In his hand the prophet laurel flowers no more.*

After such a message there he stood now to witness with his own eyes the temple of Apollo deserted, empty altogether of worshippers. And the Emperor, a faithful votary of the Olympians whose innermost thoughts were suffused with the magic of Greek philosophy, came to realize that the gods of his dreams could not be restored to life. The memory of this bitter, grieved moment no doubt returned to him later, when despair at the shattering of all his hopes wrung from his heart the cry: " Thou hast conquered, Galilean !"

However, was it true ? And to what extent ? More than fifteen centuries had already passed, and we are faced by the same question. Did Christianity entirely triumph ? Were not many of our traditions and beliefs still immersed in paganism ? A deeply suggestive story like that of Daphne lasted through its own enduring quality. For long cherished in Byzantium, it spread thence to the Balkans, where Greek influences prevailed.

And so to the present day people address short invocations:

> *Daphne, Daphne,*
> *We have dusted you,*
> *We have cared for you,*
> *Daphne. . . .*

They sit and tell of her youth ravished by impetuous Apollo; how love burned in him, and he would give her no peace; and when he forcibly embraced her, Daphne prayed to be freed and she was then changed into an oleander with strong perfume, whom one calls in songs:

> *Daphne, Daphne,*
> *We have dusted you,*
> *We have cared for you,*
> *Daphne. . . .*

XVIII. HELLENISTIC CITIES IN SYRIA

LEAVING Antioch on my return journey towards the spring of Orontes, the first town where I tarried a little was Hamah, the ancient Hamath of the Bible. As it has remained outside any Western influences, one could here see the Arabs at their ease and leisure. Time does not count for much to them. Slowly they linger in the cafés or saunter about the bazaars, intermixed with Bedouins and the even-treading camels of the desert.

Rows of houses with their old, Orontes-wetted walls present a picturesque aspect, adding to it the sight of enormous wooden wheels that creak and groan as they turn incessantly and lift the water from the river. And on its banks shadowy, veiled women come at twilight to breathe the cool air for a while.

The Greek population in Hamah must have been once very numerous; witness their metropolitan church, sunk to-day on one side, with a time-worn black façade. From its cave-like obscurity I took out a queer large icon to examine. It portrayed the High Priest of the Hebrews in the middle; on his right and left the members of the Sanhedrin, passing judgment on Christ, brought to trial before them.

Akin to Hamah there is another town upon the Orontes: Homs. Its present name does not reveal much; but if we turn to the Hellenistic one of Emesa it opens rich vistas in the past. For me it conjures up the shade of Longinus, who, in a carefully pondered style, showed us the ways to *The Sublime* in literature.

By acquiring the position of Greek professor and counsellor at the Palmyra Court he bound himself inextricably to the tragic fate of Zenobia, that wondrous queen who flitted across the historical stage like a far-distant apparition in a tale.

Dearly she paid for the desire of renouncing her foreign allegiance. Vanquished and seized, she was carried off to Rome to add spectacular brilliance to the Emperor's triumph. As for her rank and dignity, Zenobia could not complain; the conquerors held them in great esteem. For did they not chain her in fetters, not of iron, but of solid gold ?

Beyond the Orontes' spring, which is of a volcanic character, for it stops now and then, suggesting to the people the idea of a dragon drawing in all the water and pouring it forth again—

beyond the Orontes' spring the road runs into winding chasms
under a dire, empty desolation.   And, as it is about midday
and the air seems to quiver in the dazzling sun-glare, whilst I
am nearing Damascus, my mind strays back to the immortal
wayfarer of yore and to the voice he heard from out of the
fiery vision saying, " Saul, Saul, why persecutest thou Me ?"

This call from above as well as the apostle's first touch with
Christianity came to pass in Damascus, a quite Hellenistic city
then, known to the Greeks by the name of Καλλίστη, 'Most
Beautiful.'   One can see to the present day some ancient
pillars where once stood the pagan temple.   Upon its foundation a church was erected, which later became the Ommeyad
Mosque.   One of the doorways still preserves the inscription:

Η ΒΑCΙΛΙΑ CΟΥ Χ͞Ε ΒΑCΙΛΕΙΑ
ΠΑΝΤΩΝ ΤΩΝ ΑΙΟΝΩΝ ΚΑΙ
Η ΔΕCΠΟΤΙΑ CΟΥ ΕΝ ΠΑCΗ
ΓΕΝΕΑ ΚΑΙ ΓΕΝΕΑ

" Thy Kingdom, O Christ, an everlasting Kingdom and
Thy domination shall be throughout all generations."

The church had as its patron St. John the Baptist, whose
head is believed to be buried in the crypt, standing nowadays
beneath a dome, surrounded by railings of gilded bronze.

At the time of the Iconoclast outbreak it was from Damascus
that rose the most eloquent and reasoned image-defence by
the author of *Barlaam and Joasaph*.   After the downfall of
Antioch the domicile of the Orthodox Patriarchate moved
to Damascus.   Looking for it now through a maze of narrow
streets, I was glad to find a very courteous and kind patriarch.

He showed me, and left at my disposal for a few days, two
eighteenth-century Greek manuscripts: one by Athanasius
Dabbas—*History of the Antioch Patriarchs*—and the second
containing the letters of the patriarch Sylvestrus.   From both
of them I gathered much valuable information concerning the
close relations of the Syrian Church with the Orthodox world
at large.

Damascus formed part of the Decapolis, as did also Gerasa,
across the Jordan.   When you approach this latter you feel a
particular freshness in the air, the cause of which you soon
realize, for lo ! there rushes an abundance of water; and close
to it lies Gerasa, a dead city of ruins.

At the entrance you meet an arch of triumph; to the left,
on a height, the temple of Zeus.   One column only of the

peristyle stands upright against the wall, upon which weeds have climbed. Frightened partridges fly out of the sanctuary.

Nearby is the theatre, with great doorways, with a staircase leading to rows of seats, some of them reserved, as the Greek letters make plain to this day. I descend to the agora, immense, enclosed round about by fifty-six Ionic pillars; and I proceed on to the street of colonnades, over tiles which still show the ruts ground by wheels. On either side are pavements slightly raised and, from time to time, niches bare of statues. I reach a monumental fountain, mute and dry, but I recognize the sculptured mouths of beasts through which the water had splashed into the marble basin.

I gaze and try to restore in my mind and to re-people the city with its long-extinguished life. What craving for beauty possessed these men ! At the advent of Christianity they extended their masterly gifts into the adornment of churches. Some of the mosaics they left us are a delight to the eye. The city's cathedral dated from the fourth century.

It had a fountain from which once a year, on Epiphany's day, ran wine; the same miracle it displayed in former days when Dionysus used to be worshipped here. And from the disposition of the baptistry we may presume that Christian adepts passed through certain stages of initiation and symbolism, following a ritual introduced by the Eleusinian Mysteries.

It was then a time of transition. The various creeds intertwined. Longinus, in the treatise on *The Sublime* of a heathen nature, quoted alike from the Old and the New Testament. St. Gregory Nazianzen tried his best to fit Christianity into an obvious Hellenic framework; and, when the spell of the classics was too powerful to be resisted, he went back and caught the full-deep Euripidean accents in order to sing in *Christos Paschon* of the ineffable sorrows. Did not Constantine the Great himself strike coins with the head of the God Helios and the inscription *Sol invictus*?

XIX. THE MONASTERY OF MOUNT SINAI

MY arrival at Mount Sinai Monastery seemed to be a long dream. When I saw, up on the moonlit terrace, two figures of monks I stood in doubt. Were they not apparitions from another world?

A sense of unreality possessed me, even after I had entered a little door covered with iron plaques, passed through two more doors of the same kind, and continued through narrow galleries and winding staircases to the priory, where all the monks came to make me welcome.

It being rather late, and feeling more dazed than tired, I went to bed. Early next morning I stepped out on the veranda to take stock of things. Dim, overpowering and unearthly quiet, the mountain loomed up. Once it had harboured a great number of hermits. It was at their earnest demand that Justinian decided on the founding of this monastery, which, considering the far-distant isolation of Sinai, came to serve both as a shrine and a fortress.

With regard to its building, Eutychius, Alexandrian Patriarch of the tenth century, who wrote in Arabic, has left us a most peculiar story. The Emperor, he says, intended to have the monastery on the top of the mountain, and consequently he dispatched to Sinai a commissioner, who, however, altered the Emperor's design, building the monastery in the valley, where it is to-day. When the commissioner returned to Byzantium and presented Justinian with a report of his finished work, the Emperor asked: "Why did you not build the monastery on the mountain-top, as I wanted?"

"Because," he replied, "the bush and the water are down below; had they been touched, the monks would have died of thirst up there."

"Then I expected you to cut down the mountain to the level of the bush and water."

"Were we to spend all the revenues of the Roman Empire, of Syria and Egypt, we still could not accomplish such a thing."

Whereupon Justinian became very angry and ordered the commissioner to be executed.

So from the start the monastery had comprised within its precincts the site where the miraculous bush burned with unconsuming fire. Out of it God for the first time revealed to

Moses His name as The Self-existing, translated by ὁ ῎Ων, which
is always found in the halo of our Lord's picture. As Moses
walked towards the bush there spoke the Almighty: " Moses,
Moses ! draw not nigh hither; put off thy shoes from thy
feet. . . ."

Answering the same call, I too approached barefoot towards
what is nowadays called in the Church Ἁγία Βάτος. A lamp
burns here unquenched for centuries, and for centuries likewise
the incense-clouded prayers have ascended from here. Above,
on the apse, a mosaic of the Transfiguration shines with
subdued lustre. To think that it dates from Justinian's reign
and that it exhibits a noble mastery in Byzantine art, as do
indeed other things around me of the same period—the
solemn, granite columns, the carved wood ceiling, the pavement in marble traceries of different colours !

Close by the altar I see the relics of St. Catherine. Hailing
from Cyprus, this saint met with martyrdom at Alexandria,
and the angels carried her bones on to a peak of Sinai, whereabouts exactly nobody knew; but intimation came through a
dream vision to one of the pious fathers of the monastery.
Then all proceeded to fetch the holy relics and bear them in
reverent procession down to the church.

It came about that the monks suffered a terrible thirst upon
the arid path. What else could they do but sink on their knees
and pray ? Behold, immediately a partridge beat its wings
above in the air and sprinkled them with water. The monks
understood at once, and, following the flight of the bird, they
found a spring, which they still call the Spring of the Partridge.

The superior of the monastery, Archbishop Porphirios, a
most kind and saintly man, led me to various chapels and afterwards to the library, connected with many a reputed work and
author. I took my fill of enjoyment, starting with Cosmas
Indicopleustes, a wandering merchant who, after having
travelled on land and sea throughout Egypt and beyond it, in
Ethiopia, India, Ceylon, settled down to a cloistered life and
wrote his Χριστιανικὴ Τοπογραφία, Christian Topography, about
the year A.D. 547. Educated in Alexandria, he was acquainted
with Byzantine illumination art as then practised, and used
it for a new purpose—to illustrate with a sure hand whatever
strange material he had gathered during his extensive journeys.

Not long after Cosmas Indicopleustes, towards the close of
the sixth century, there came to be head of the Sinai Monastery
John Climax, so named because he was responsible for the
Greek Κλίμαξ, a Spiritual Ladder, showing the gradual steps

one has to mount in order to reach perfection. Though, according to a prevailing custom, his virtues and vices are personified embodiments, he works the latter together into scenes at once vivid and minutely depicted. Gregory Nazianzen is represented by a twelfth-century of the Homilies which quite befits the excellence of his text.

Numerous other parchment rarities passed under my eyes. While engrossed in them, smiling at the lines often recurring in the end, " Whoever at any time removes or takes this script from the monastery, let him be ranked with Satan and incur the anathema of all the Nicæan Synod's Fathers," I heard the voice of Archbishop Porphirios say, rather scornfully:

" And here is the Codex Sinaiticus !" He drew my attention to a folio in uncial Greek letters. " Yes," he said, " the Codex Sinaiticus. On behalf of the Tsar they had asked to borrow the manuscript for a short while to copy it only at St. Petersburg, and then return it to us. And look what they have done; instead of the original, they have sent us this, which is a copy."

In a lecture delivered at the British Museum during the time they were collecting the money for the acquisition of the Codex Sinaiticus, I repeated exactly what Archbishop Porphirios told me—a harmless statement that turned out, however, to be alarming. Some of the newspapers, which judged things solely by material standards and did not approve of the Government spending money for a manuscript, seized on the above words for a further opposition. At my second lecture, therefore, I had to read a letter of the British Museum authorities giving the facts as related by Tischendorf. Though I could hardly believe Tischendorf's story, I did not personally take up an attitude on the matter, but happening to again meet Archbishop Porphirios in Cairo, I reopened the subject. " Tischendorf," I said, " refers to a sum advanced for the manuscript."

" I know," answered Archbishop Porphirios, " but that was a simple donation for our kindness in allowing the manuscript to be taken out of the monastery. I have all the documents to prove that we never gave away or sold to anyone the Codex Sinaiticus. I intended to bring the matter before the courts; but then, I thought, what success could we have, who is going to listen to us, poor monks of the desert ?"

After midday I began the ascent of the mountain, three thousand one hundred steps cut out of the rock. As I went the monastery came more and more into the picture, a whole view of it. Before any change in the landscape I encountered a chapel, dedicated to St. Mary, of no other interest than for its quaint legend.

On one occasion the famished monks decided to close the monastery, and had walked out on to the mountain for a last service. In their path, just at the spot where the chapel is now, a woman appeared: "Why do you go when food is arriving?" As soon as she had spoken she vanished, a happening at which the monks wondered greatly. But when they returned they saw camels with a load of corn entering the monastery. Who could the unknown have been if not the Virgin Mary herself?

At a distance from the chapel are two stone arches. In the old days they served as some kind of holy stations. Pilgrims used to stop under them and confess that they might proceed with cleansed, unburdened souls. Now the path turned and narrowed between steep cliffs. At the top, over the barren ridge, there emerged, silhouetted on the skies, a cypress tree. How utterly forlorn and solitary! For what long years it must have stood thus, dreaming of green companions! It guarded a cell, once belonging to a hermit, now empty. Also empty was, to the left, Elijah's cave, except for a picture much similar to one of Cosmas Indicopleustes' miniatures: a young Moses receives the decalogue from a hand stretched forth from heaven.

A little farther, and I found myself on the summit of Mount Sinai—a unique moment resembling nothing else in life. As far as the eye could reach the whole was solid granite beneath the last flames of the sunset. Great mountain beyond mountain stood motionless in purple magnificence. The silence that had impressed me all the way up was complete here, supernatural, overwhelming. Nothing stirred, not a living thing. Only the wind, and in it I recognized the voice of God.

PART II
ORTHODOXY IN THE BALKANS

I

THE oldest people in the Balkans were: the Greeks, more numerous along the sea-coast; the Illyrians, whose descendants are the present-day Albanians; and the Thraco-Dacians. The latter, having intermingled with a strong element of Roman colonists, gave birth to a Latin-speaking population known as the Rumanians. In the sixth century the Slavs penetrated from Asia, followed some time after by the Bulgarians. Both settled amongst the Rumanians, dividing them in two: those north of the Danube, and the Vlachs, spread over Macedonia, Epirus, and Thessaly.

Of Hun origin, but gradually Slavonized, the Bulgarians succeeded in forming a state of their own, which gained some fame under the Tsar Boris in the second half of the ninth century, when they adopted Christianity. Their conversion brought to light the keen rivalry between the Churches of Rome and Byzantium—both of which laid claim to spiritual suzerainty over Bulgaria. The Bulgarians chose Greek Orthodoxy, and developed a remarkable culture, especially under Boris' immediate successor, Tsar Simeon.

As one who studied in Byzantium, he tried to emulate its learning and its sumptuous life. He enriched the aspect of his own capital, Preslav, and directly assisted the translation of numerous outstanding works from Greek into Bulgarian. These cultural endeavours matched the pace of his resounding conquests; so much so that, flushed by victories, he assumed the title of Emperor of the Romans and Bulgarians alike. (By Romans being understood here all the subjects of Byzantium.) When, however, in the summer of 924 he met the Byzantine Emperor, Romanus Lecapenus, legend says that two eagles appeared above the monarchs' heads, hovered awhile in the air, then one made for Byzantium, the other flew towards Thrace. Simeon might have seen in this a portent of his unlikely chance of ever becoming the sole overlord.

The less ambitious title of Basileus was given to Simeon's heir, Peter, by the Emperor Romanus Lecapenus, whose granddaughter he married. It was then, through the clause of a treaty, that an autonomous Bulgarian Patriarchate came to be recognized. But soon after Bulgaria fell entirely under the rule of Byzantium, lasting up to the turning of the twelfth century, when the Bulgarians, stirred and aided by the Vlachs, sprang again into prominence, mainly thanks to their leader Joannitza. No less than Simeon he aimed at a high imperial fame. During the time of his successors Bulgaria's cultural tendencies revived and steadily continued until the advent of the Turks.

We get a vivid glimpse of Serbia in the year 918, when the Byzantine Empress Zoe, unable to cope alone with Simeon's attacks, prevailed upon Serbia to join in the fight against the Bulgarians.

In Serbia there existed a number of more or less autonomous organizations, led by Jupan chiefs, which Stephen, the founder of the Nemanja dynasty, succeeded in welding together. By the second half of the twelfth century, as a result of the missionary zeal of Cyril and Methodius, the Serbs had adopted Christianity and entered the sphere of Byzantium. But the people of Croatia and the Dalmatian coast refused to accept the Slavonic liturgy and submitted to Catholic influences. This had for long remained an obstacle to the unity of Yugoslavia.

The Nemanjas reached the zenith of their achievements under Stephen Dušan, who had himself crowned Emperor of the Romans and Serbs in 1346, and established an autocephalus patriarchate in the town of Ipek. Moreover, the beneficent religious intercourse with Byzantium continued to give an impetus to the folk-products and art, as manifested to-day in the lofty monasteries with their treasures of wall painting, icons and reliquaries, until it was checked by the battle of Kossovo in 1389. Although the Serbs lost the battle, it remained throughout the centuries an inspiration to them, and Serb epic has imparted a mystical sense to this defeat. Serb legend has it that when the warrior king prepared for battle, a grey falcon from Jerusalem appeared in the sky and spoke these words:

> *Say, dost thou desire a heavenly Kingdom,*
> *Or an earthly Kingdom dost thou prefer?*

And, as Lazar chose the heavenly, the grey falcon announced that he and his army would have to perish at Kossovo. It is the idea of redemption. They sacrificed themselves so that Serbia might live a life of honour and liberty. That is why Serbs in times of adversity drew from it not only solace, but also strength and hope for the destiny of their nation.

The battle of Kossovo took place twenty-nine years after

the fall of Adrianople, which left a vague far-away echo in the Greek folk-song:

Lament the nightingales of Wallachia and the birds in the West. . . .

The verse alludes to the Thessalian Wallachia, at that time in decline, while a new Wallachia and later Moldavia rose on the other side of the Danube. Both provinces depended ecclesiastically on Byzantium, whence came the inspiration as well as the material that was to be gradually woven into a pattern of rich native culture. Among the princes who lent splendour to their rule were Mircea the Old, Stephen the Great, and the meteor-like Michael the Brave, who in 1600 for a brief period united all the Rumanian provinces.

II

MANY writers on the subject of the Balkan Peninsula had dealt with one or other of its peoples separately, without considering their common ties and features, due first of all to pagan influences.

A pale reminiscence of sacrificing a human being at the erection of an important work still lingers in a ballad *The Master Builder*, current throughout the Balkans. Indeed, the Albanians connect it with a bridge in the town of Dibra; the Bulgarians with Salonica; the Greeks as well as the Vlachs with the bridge of Arta; the Serbs with Skadar or Scutary; and the Rumanians with the Argesh Monastery. The sacrifice, however, of a lamb or of a cock persists to this day and it takes place on various occasions. There is on the Pindus mountain a village by the name of Perivole, whose inhabitants pray to an old icon of St. George at a stone altar:

" Mighty St. George, take us under thy protection, help us and we will bring to thee the fattest of the lambs."

After which they descend the mountain. As many flocks and herds as they encounter they forcibly drive towards the Warm Valley, covered with dense forest, where all trace of them is lost. And on the return they revel before the saint, songs and dances and sacrifices are offered, the number of which depends upon the success of the raid.

Rebecca West, who recently published an exhaustingly brilliant book on Yugoslavia, *Black Lamb and Grey Falcon*, witnessed in that country a black lamb presented as sacrifice at a certain stone—an act propitiatory to the begetting of children. The occasion prompted her to some reflections, which, coming from the author of *St. Augustine*, are profound and sincere; they do not attempt to explain the rite itself. " Women," says Rebecca West, " do not get children by the slaughter of a lamb, the breaking of a jar. . . ." No, indeed; but people do not stay to think or question about a practice forming part of a long tradition. That particular sacrificial stone was probably connected with a pagan worship of Venus.

On the way to the Vlach village of Clisura in Macedonia I know of a solitary, huge rock among some birch-trees, named the Rock-with-icon, where for untold centuries maidens and wives proceed in the early morning. With oil jars in their hands, humbly they approach the Rock-with-icon and enter a cave one by one. Here, beneath the flickering light of candles, a saintly figure is revealed, carved indistinctly out of the cave's wall. Girls and women bow; then, falling on hands and knees, they struggle in turn through a black, narrow passage which brings them out again into the light behind the cave, where one hears coming from each: " May it help you ! May it help you !" A wish for a speedy marriage, or an easy confinement. This stone was an altar, dedicated in old times to the powerful goddess of love and nativity, whom we find nowadays travestied in Christian garbs under the name of St. Paraskiva, a saint greatly favoured by the female sex. One of the oldest churches in Salonica, dating from the fifth century, which the Turks used to call Eski Djuma, is dedicated to St. Paraskiva and is known to have been erected on the site of a temple to Aphrodite.

One has to bear in mind that Macedonia had inspired Euripides' *Bacchae* and that generally the Balkans were renowned for the practice of mystical rites. These had struck so deep a root in tradition that they could not be easily forsaken.

A folk-poem, for instance, going by the name of *Mioritza*, withstood, like a magic flower, all the winds of centuries. It savours of pastoral life on high solitary places. A little black ewe, the pet of the flock, discloses to her master the secret that two of his associates have planned to kill him. The shepherd does not seem to take any measures to prevent the murder. In a mood of resigned fatalism he only gives instructions as to what is to be done if he dies. He wishes to be buried by the sheepfold, and near to his head are to be placed his three flutes, the flute of birchwood, the flute of bone, and the flute of reeds, so that the wind blowing through them may strike forth sweet melodies. Further, he does not want it to be known that he was murdered, but only that he was married to a beautiful Queen, the bride of the world.

A similar conception of death appears in a Greek ballad, *The Farewell of the Clepht*, the translation of which runs as follows:

> *Do not say I perished, that I died—poor me !*
> *Say only that I wedded in the lone foreign land,*
> *That I took the tombstone for mother-in-law,*
> *The black earth for my wife. . . .*

Both in richness of imagery and in the choice of words making for exquisite cadences, the Rumanian *Mioritza* attains to a very high literary level. The shepherd speaks to the ewe:

"But thou, do not tell them of the murder; tell them only that I have married a beautiful Queen, the bride of the world; that at my wedding a star fell. The sun and the moon held my chaplets. For wedding guests, I had the fir-trees, and the aspens. For priests, the lofty mountains; the birds for minstrels —thousands of birds—and the stars for torches."

Strange words these. In their rich imagery we catch some inner meaning of the Elusinian legends. The mystic nuptials, in which all nature takes a share, are but those of the under-world's goddess with Adonis, himself a youth of lonely pastures and beautiful withal, just like the hero of our ballad. His mother, who runs across the fields, is identified in many carols with Lady Mary. Wearing the black robes of a nun she wanders on the Judean hills in search of her Son. Everything seems transfixed under an ominous silence. No soul anywhere. At the waters of Jordan she encounters the godfather of Jesus:

> *Listen, John,*
> *St. John !*
> *Hast thou seen*
> *Or hast thou heard*
> *Of my Son,*
> *The Lord of Heaven*
> *And of earth ?*

St. John tells her what he himself has heard concerning the crucifixion, and advises her to go to the fountain of Pilate if she wishes to get a glimpse of her Son. Mary continues moaning aloud and

> *Where her tears fall*
> *Golden apples grow;*
> *Where her feet tread*
> *Rich crops spring forth. . . .*

In the image of Mary, who does not recognize that of the ancient goddess of fertility? What is given here in the form of narrative verse is dramatically performed on the Eve of St. John. A girl dressed up in bridal attire and carrying in her hands a brazen, flower-bedecked jug, is taken to three fountains in turn, while the company around begins a stereotypic Vlach song which makes no sense whatever:

> *Stravo votane, stravo coinare. . . .*

It is in reality a corruption of the Greek:

> σταβρὸ ἀπὸ βοτάνη, σταβρὸ ἀπὸ κλονάρη. . . .
> *Cross of a plant, cross of a branch. . . .*

And, as one goes through the quaint details of a wedding ceremony, another song is heard telling of a symbolical union of the girl to a god, be he Adonis or Dionysus or any other who has not yet lost touch with the people.

The survival of this ancient, deeply significant conception appears even clearer in the Balkanic Hobby-horse dance, containing in it all the elements of a Dionysian ritual. The ethnological museum at Sofia displays the costumes and implements used by the Hobby-horse dance.

III

FROM an early date the Balkans were permeated by
various heresies. The Byzantine Emperor, Constantine
Copronymos, brought into Thrace from Asia a good
number of Manichæans. Out of them in the tenth century
there rose a priest, Jeremiah, who called himself Bogomil—
corresponding to the Greek Theophilos, Friend of God—
who preached a doctrine founded on the continuous, unrelent-
ing antagonism between God and Satanael. His adherents
made extensive use of the Apocrypha and of such legendary
episodes of the Bible which could appeal to the imagination
of the people; of course, amplifying and embellishing them, to
suit better their purpose. For instance, when Adam is expelled
from the blessed garden, we hear him lamenting: "Paradise,
oh, splendid Paradise, beauty ineffable, created for my sake
and now shut to me for evermore! . . ." Again, seeing the
approach of death, Adam is seized with a great longing for
the fruit of Paradise, and sends his son Seth to fetch it. Seth
proceeds on the journey. After many hardships, having escaped
from a hideous wild beast, he arrives at the gate of Paradise
and informs Archangel Michael of his errand.

"Fruit?" asks the Archangel. "There is no fruit on the
Tree of Knowledge any more."

But, with God's benevolent permission, the Archangel gives
him a branch of the tree. Seth brings it to Adam, who dies
with a deep sigh, taking it with him to the grave. From that
branch a marvellous tree grew, out of which the crucifix was
made.

Now, at the death of Adam, a host of angels descended with
lighted torches and prayed God to receive his soul. Then a
voice came from above: "Adam, Adam! Remember what
I have once said: Earth thou art, and unto earth thou shalt
return."

Each great event of the Bible is dealt with in the light of a
strong dualism, Satanael opposing God. Interlaced with it,
one comes across numerous legends, such as that of the Virgin
Mary. Very popular, spread also beyond the Balkans, it was
introduced by Dostoevsky in his novel *The Brothers Karamazov.*
Mary is led by the Archangel Michael into hell, where she
sees the appalling torments of the sinners. She could not help

weeping out of overwhelming pity for them all. She kneels down at the throne of God and prays for mercy. Whereupon the Almighty grants a certain respite to the sufferers.

In like manner strange dreams and visions are given, as one can see better in Macarius the Hermit's *Bulgarian Sinodicon*, all being connected with the soul's journey to the netherworld and to the Last Judgement. Stress likewise is laid on pieces of attractive folklore, in which one might detect the promptings of an evil spirit; such, for instance, the Rumanian poem, *The Cuckoo and the Turtle-Dove*.

Sweet turtle-dove, little white bird, let us love together!
I should like to, but I fear your mother.
She is a witch, and she would scold and scold. . . .
Dear little turtle-dove, little white bird, do come and be my love!
No, cuckoo, no! Ask me no more; for to be left alone I will turn
*   into a reed.*
If you turn into a reed, I will change myself into a shepherd.
I will find you and make a flute of the reed that I may play on it and
*   kiss it.*
No, cuckoo, no! I cannot listen to you.
Ah, if it were not for your mother!
But rather than be with her, I would become a saint's image in church.
Even then I will follow you.
I will change into a deacon,
And there, in the church, will bow to you and worship you, saying:
Little saint's image, turn into a bird,
And let us love and be together.

There is in Serbian a variant of this poem, in which human beings take the place of birds. A curious little song of the same category, found on the Pindus region, tells both in Greek and in Rumanian about a Turk who had cast an evil eye on a Vlach girl. She in order to escape from him would change successively into a lamb, a partridge, a hind, a fish, a flower; but the Turk in his turn would pursue her everywhere as a shepherd, an eagle, and so forth, repeating obstinately all the time:

Κόρη μ' θὰ σὲ πάρω,
Κόρη μ' δὲν σέ-αφίνω!

I will take you, my girl;
I will not leave you!

IV

PAGAN legends, queer superstitions, fanciful heresies—all penetrated the rich texture of Christianity, which came to the Balkan nations in the shape of Byzantine Orthodoxy. It meant a particular culture, comprising art, literature, theology, in the service of the Church.

The Balkan nations inherited from Byzantium the institution of absolute ruler, the Lord's anointed. The ambitious among them craved for the title of Emperor, which some obtained from the Pope in view of certain proselytizing aims, and others usurped it themselves. Such were the cases of the Bulgarian Simeon, Dušan the Serb and Vladislav, a Wallachian Prince of the fourteenth century, who is represented in an icon of St. Athanasius, presented to the Lavra Monastery on Mount Athos as calling himself Autocrat.

The Court ceremonial and various manifestations in the life of sovereigns and people were imbued with a Christian orthodox spirit, which entered and coloured even political intercourses. A startling example is the meeting of the Emperor Romanus Lecapenus with Simeon, the Bulgarian Tsar I, referred to before. In his triumphant advance Simeon comes within sight of Byzantium. Awed, it appears, by the magnificent city, he asks for an interview with the Emperor. After a prayer at the Blachernæ Church, and attired in the solemn ecclesiastical cloak, Romanus goes to encounter Simeon, whom he addresses thus:

" I have heard that you are a religious man and a devoted Christian; but I do not see your acts harmonizing with your words. A religious Christian welcomes peace and love, for it is said of God to be love; it is a godless and un-Christian man who rejoices in slaughter and shedding of innocent blood. If then you are a true Christian—since you claim to be a Christian—you do not desire to stain Christian hands with the blood of fellow-Christians. You are a mortal; you await death and resurrection and judgement. To-day you live, and to-morrow you are dust; one fever will quench all your pride. What will you say, when you go before God, of your unrighteous slaughter ? How will you face the terrible, just Judge ? . . ."

One cannot understand such a speech in the mouth of the

Emperor, if one does not pay heed to the intellectual atmosphere of the time. John Curcuas, a capable general of the same Emperor Lecapenus, had laid siege in 942 to the city of Edessa, where was preserved the Agbar portrait of Christ. In order to obtain it, Curcuas made peace with the Moslems and released a number of their prisoners. And when the sacred image solemnly entered Byzantium, it brought to General Curcuas a greater fame than all his many successes put together.

Then one has to consider the books that formed the everyday spiritual nourishment of those days. I mean other than ecclesiastical books, such as *Barlaam and Joasaph*, *Alexander the Great*, *Phisiologus*, *Lives of the Saints*. They were not many; but what wisdom accumulated in them ! What influential potency ! The more so as they constituted a constant reading for the people of those days.

Intertwined with quaint Eastern tales, which enhance the charm of the work, *Barlaam and Joasaph* pleads the renouncing of worldly things and the preparing for a life beyond. In the romance of *Alexander the Great* there are not only many ancient Christian legends introduced, but the hero himself is made to speak the Christian tongue. The *Phisiologus* takes various beasts and birds in which certain Christian virtues are embodied, and tries to force them upon the attention of its readers.

And, as the transitory nature of life and its swift shadow-like passage is constantly emphasized, a profound sorrow underlies all these books; and through them all is heard, like a recurring, unescapable refrain, the words of the author of Ecclesiastes: " Vanity of vanities, all is vanity."

About the *Lives of the Saints*, what should I say ? Notwithstanding its odd mixture of reality and fancy, how many did not try to imitate its contents by withdrawing from active life ? Boris, the first Christian King of Bulgaria, at the height of a striking reign, abdicated in favour of his son, taking the road to a solitary penitence. So did Stephen Nemanja the Serb, followed by his wife, who also entered a convent; whilst her third son returned from Mount Athos, where he had assumed a monarch's name of Saba, to become Serbia's first Archbishop. After him John Uroš, son of King Simeon, took the habit and under the name of Joasaph joined the Blessed Athanasius in the foundation of the first shrine on the rocks of Meteora, dedicated to the Transfiguration at the outset of the fourteenth century. And one could see there to-day numerous letters and charters from Simeon Uroš, from Dušan and from Joasaph's sister, wife of Thomas Preliubovič, Despot of Ianina, who calls herself Maria Anghelini Duca Paleologou. All are signed in red ink, as the Emperors of Byzantium used to do. In Wallachia too, Vlad the Monk and Radou Paisius left the cloister in order to mount a worldly throne. Those among kings, princes and nobles who did not succumb to the call of retirement used to vie with each other in building or endowing churches, irrespective of nationality, as faith then stood above anything else; though many of them felt a deep, hidden need to atone for sins in which they profusely indulged. And in the donation-charters as a rule they specified the days when alms were to be given and prayers offered for the good of their souls.

CHRIST CHURCH OF ST. SOPHIA, OCHRIDA; XITH CENTURY

(Facing p. 92)

A SAINT PAINTED BY ZUKI OF EPIRUS;
HOLY TRINITY CHURCH, METEORA

(Facing p. 93)

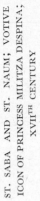

ST. PARASKIVA, WALLACHIAN ICON

ST. SABA AND ST. NAUM; VOTIVE
ICON OF PRINCESS MILITZA DESPINA;
XVIITH CENTURY

V

THE oldest Balkan churches, save for those in Istanbul, are to be found in Greece, Bulgaria and Serbia. It was from the latter country that Nicodemus, a worthy member of the clergy, crossed the Danube into Wallachia to found monasteries, where only humble wooden shrines had existed before. The earlier Orthodox monument in Rumania to-day is the Princely Church of Argesh, dating from the first half of the fourteenth century. It displays obvious resemblance to churches of the same period in the Balkans, such as Trapezitza and Peter-Paul of Trnovo in Bulgaria, and Lesnovo and Nageriča in Serbia. They all could be related to a Byzantine type represented by the Chora, now the Kahrié Djami at Istanbul.

Masons and painters came from south of the Danube, where genuine Byzantine art was fostered in the secluded monasteries of the highlands of Thrace, Macedonia and Epirus. Out of many treasures existing at the Holy Sepulchre the choicest is a little illuminated ninth-century script of the Book of Job, deriving from Melenic. An English traveller, J. F. Abbott, who visited that town in the year 1900, wrote as follows:

" At St. Stephen's I was shown three large folio manuscripts of the Gospels, written on fine parchment and bound in solid wood-boards. One of them was richly illuminated. . . . In the same church there are preserved some magnificent bishops' vestments, lavishly embroidered with gold and coloured silk. One of them had the genealogical tree of Jesse wrought in these materials down the front, each branch bearing a cluster of rosy patriarchs and prophets. The delicate finish of detail and tasteful grouping of the figures and colours evinced the art of no mean artist, whoever he was."

From the twelfth century onwards Mount Athos began to play its conspicuous part, evolving a somewhat new kind of Byzantine art, less hieratic, animated by the freer breath of the Renaissance and the talent of Greek painters like Panselinos and Theophanes, who had accomplished such brilliant work at the monasteries. On a liturgical fan, dated 1488 and now found at Patmos, one reads the following inscription:

> *I, Stephen Voevod by the grace of God,*
> *Hospodar of Moldavia, made this at the*
> *Zographou monastery of Mount Athos.*

It means there existed at Zographou—as undoubtedly must have existed at the Serbian Chilandari and at the Greek monasteries—groups of trained and recognized craftsmen. They and their many pupils used to receive orders at the monastery or travel the length and breadth of the Balkans to carry out their commissions. To this fact we owe the excellent products of enchanting similarity admired in the portraits of the Bulgarian Bojana Monastery and the Trnovo churches; in the Serbian St. Clement Church of Ochrida and in the monasteries Gračanica and Kalenič; in the Wallachian Princely Church and in the numerous Gospel miniatures.

We have to picture all this against a background of inter-mixed races, which were confused even by Byzantine writers who could not tell them apart. As Catrari, writing in the fourteenth century, put it: " Do you want to know what he is? Vlach he is by birth; Albanian by appearance; and by his manner Bulgar-Albanian-Greek." In some cases the idea of collectivity is developed still further by the inclusion of the Serb; a certain despot of Epirus, for example, was said to have been a Serb-Albanian-Bulgar-Vlach—ἀρβαλβανίτοβουλγαρόβλαχος. This is the outside view; upon closer examination, however, we discern in each group of the agglomeration a latent sense of nationality, which now and then comes to the surface. At the outset of the thirteenth century King Joannitza in his letters to Pope Innocent III affirms as a Vlach his connection with Rome, no matter for what ulterior purpose. Princess Militza Despina, though the wife of Voevod Neagoe Bessarab, does not forget her Serbian descent, and in a beautiful votive icon we see her praying to the patron saints of Serbia, St. Saba and St. Naum. When in 1676 a certain Guma builds a monastery at the island of Ianina and attaches to it a school, he does it as a Greek for the good of the Greeks. We detect the sense of nationality even at closer contacts, strengthened by intermarriages, as happened to be the case in the fourteenth century with Bessarab I, the Wallachian Voevod, who gave his daughter Theodora to Tsar Alexander of Bulgaria; while the latter's sister was taken to wife by the great Dušan—a family alliance of three Balkan rulers, made for mutual assistance. At the time of Kossovo, Mircea the Old sent an army, which fought and perished side by side with the Serbian. And a Rumanian legend says that, when the same Mircea was attacked by the Turks, Kralievič Marco of Serbia hastened to his help, and before the battle he prayed to God that he should die for the defence of Christianity.

At the princely courts of both countries favourite minstrels used to sing of Serb and Wallachian heroes alike; and popular figures, like Michael the Brave, were extolled in all the Balkan tongues. A manuscript of such a Greek folk-poem exists at the Simopetra Monastery on Mount Athos.

VI

A SENSIBLE change in the Balkans followed the Turkish invasion. The truth is, the Turks did not possess a culture of their own to bestow or impose upon the subdued Christians; they influenced only their manners of life—and not everywhere to the same extent. One has to make a distinction between the Danubian provinces and the countries south of the Danube. In these latter territories the marks left by the Turks are much deeper. At Ianina I saw houses which still show an interior balcony, closed on all sides save for a hole through which the maiden of the house managed to obtain a glimpse of the man chosen by the parents to be her future husband. Many churches preserve to this day a special gallery for women, and girls are generally kept in seclusion. In the remote mountain villages, if you happen to be seen by a group of girls who are sitting talking on the threshold, they will fly at once to hide themselves like frightened birds. But as you pass on, you are intensely conscious of their warm glances from behind a window or slightly opened door. A youth can but rarely meet a young girl by herself, except at an occasional festival or during those dusky hours after sunset when she hurries to fetch water from the fountain. Then a mere hand-clasp makes for entire happiness; their lips draw together, and the long-wished-for kiss is so exquisitely sweet that even the stars cannot help noticing it.

Κόρη, ὄντας φιλιώμασταν κήντα ἦτον ποιὸς μᾶσ εἶδε. . . .

Thus begins a beautiful Greek song with variants in other Balkan tongues. I give it in translation:

> My girl, when we kissed each other
> It was night, who could see us?
> The night did, the stars, the moon;
> And she whispered to the sea.
> To the oar the sea. The oar
> Told a sailor, and he soon
> Sang it in a song ashore
> At my beloved's door.

Then in face of the Turkish onrush the prevalent social order had broken down altogether. Many people were forced to seek a way of living or a haven elsewhere, generally on the other side of the Danube. A folk-poem of Zagori in Epirus speaks about the young men who are

> *Twelve years in Wallachia*
> *And three nights at their home.*

A Bulgarian song runs: .

> *Thin drops of rain fall like pearls,*
> *My beloved saddles his horse*
> *To depart and become rich*
> *In Wallachia.*

What was it that made both Wallachia and Moldavia so much sought after?

Recent English publicists, under the influence of present-day political tendencies inculcated by the war, tried to belittle the achievements of the Danubian provinces; nay, the latter were presented as if they had never enjoyed but a kind of fictitious liberty. "The Turks," said one, "brought an end of Rumanian semi-independencies." Another stated in a trenchant manner that, after the battle of Mohacs in 1526, "for the next four hundred years Eastern Europe was ruled by three great Empires: Austria and the Ottoman Empire in the south, and in the north Poland until the end of the eighteenth century, and afterwards Russia. These great States swallowed up the smaller nations, which do not appear again till modern times. . . . The battle of Mohacs ended the cultural development of the Danubian peoples, as the fall of Constantinople had ended that of the Balkan peoples."

The truth is the Danubian Principalities, owing to historical circumstances and to their geographical position, were spared the yoke of the Turks, who had not even the right to build a mosque in either of the provinces. Once when Miron Costin, the Rumanian chronicler, had been sent on a political errand to the Grand Vizier, who was then encamping on the Dniester, the latter asked him whether the Moldavians were glad of the Turkish conquests. Miron Costin replied: "Glad are we, the Moldavians, that the Turkish Empire should spread as much in any direction, but over our own country we are not glad to see it spread." The Vizier then laughed and said: "You have spoken well!" So long as the Sultan could get a tribute, he allowed the rulers of the Danubian provinces full initiative and liberty. What better proof that one of them, Peter, Voevod of Moldavia, signed in 1588 a treaty with England, as

7

related by William Hareborne, an agent of Queen Elizabeth to Turkey. Arriving from Constantinople in Iassy, he met with most courteous reception from Peter the Voevod, " with whom was concluded that her Maiesties subjects there trafiquing should pay but three upon the hundredth which as well his owne subjects as all other nations answere: whose letters to her Maiestie be extant." He gives the Latin text of " the privilege of Peter the Prince of Moldavia," the earliest treaty between England and Rumania.

For a long period the two Principalities were fortunate to possess a succession of capable, high-minded rulers, who realized that, after the downfall of Constantinople, to them fell the task of aiding the religious communities of Eastern Orthodoxy. In a relatively peaceful reign Matthew Bessarab lavishly assisted the cultural endeavours of Wallachia. His numerous gift-gospels are to be seen to-day at the Treasury of the Holy Sepulchre, at the Metropolitan Church of Cairo, at the Byzantine Museum, Athens; all finely done in parchment by the most skilful miniaturists of the Balkans. Basile Lupu, the Moldavian Voevod, came to be reckoned as the supreme lay head of the churches. When the Holy Sepulchre was on the verge of being lost to Orthodoxy because of the great debts incurred, it was Basile Lupu who saved it. And Dositheus, alluding to this act of pious generosity, said in his book *About the Patriarchs of Jerusalem*: " Since the loss of Constantinople nor King nor prince had done such good to the Patriarchal Throne of Jerusalem." As for Constantine Brancovan, he reached in Wallachia the hey-days of Byzantine splendour. At one time it was owing to him that the official letters of Lord Paget, British Ambassador at Constantinople, could be forwarded to England. Brancovan felt proud of the service he was thus able to render the British Government and, in referring to this, Lord Paget points out in a report how flattered the Prince would be to have a letter written to him in Latin by that Government. Thus Lord Paget knew beforehand the prince by whom he was to be received with great distinction in Wallachia. And Edmund Chishull, who had been for three years chaplain at Smyrna and accompanied Lord Paget in his homeward journey, has left us a lengthy account of their interview and of the entertainment they had in the palace of the Prince Joannes Constantinus Bassarabas, as he calls him. A passage in his very interesting *Travels* gives the reader a glimpse of the country's progress at that time, the year 1702:

" The Patriarch lodges in a large *Kane*, built by the present

Prince; where are large apartments and magazines for merchants, the rent of which may yield about twenty purses *per annum*, and is by the Prince consigned into that Patriarch's hands for the use of the Holy Sepulchre."

The Patriarch referred to here was the learned Chrysantus Notaras. His predecessor Dositheus had already established a printing press at Iassy; whilst another one was working in Bucharest, under the care of Athanasius Dabbas, Patriarch of Antioch and a Georgian monk Anthimus. Many pieces of devotion in Arabic saw the light here for the benefit of the Christian population in Syria.

It is therefore a belatedly erroneous idea still persisting among British historians that the Phanariot epoch was one of ignorance and spoliation. The Ghicas, the Mavrocordatos, the Mavroghenis, the Sutzos, were all enlightened Princes, who cared much indeed for the welfare of the Rumanian provinces. In special Nicolas Mavrocordato had founded at his own monastery of Vacaresti one of the greatest libraries in Europe, containing rare manuscripts such as the *Demonstratio Evangelica* by Eusebius; Johannes Lydus' *De Magistratibus Reipublicae Romanae*, unique, now at the National Library of Paris; *The Psalms of David*, dating from the eleventh century, in white parchment with golden initial letters and minutely painted headpieces, in my possession.

It was partly during the reign of the Phanariots that the seeds of the later movements of Balkan liberation were sown in the Danubian provinces.

VII

ONE may ask, "How is it that the Balkan peoples, who have lived in practically the same conditions, under the equally strong Byzantine influences, and have so much in common, did not unite for their own good?" The answer is that only very few of their rulers were wise enough to turn a deaf ear to the mischievous instigations from outside. The Serbs were deceived by the Empress Zoe to join her war against the Bulgarians. The Byzantine chroniclers are quite definite on this point. The Bulgarians afterwards retaliated. The kings of the two Slav nations fought many battles against each other. They had primitive ideas of making wars of conquests. In the course of time one or the other got the upper hand. Simeon, the Bulgarian, gained sway over a great part of the Balkans. Three centuries later, in 1230, John Assan II recorded with pride at the Forty Martyrs' Church of Trnovo: "I have conquered all lands from Adrianople to Durazzo: Greek, Albanian and Serb land." But later the King of Serbia, Dušan, in turn subdued the Bulgarians.

Moreover, each one of them cherished the supreme desire of overthrowing Byzantium, uniting it to his dominions and proclaiming himself Autocrat of all the Balkans. This dream, which none of them could fulfil, was taken over, when the power of the Turks began to decline, by the Courts of St. Petersburg and Vienna. In this rivalry, the Russian Tsar, however, had the advantage of sharing the Orthodox faith with the Balkan people. Russia adopted a patronizing attitude towards all the Christian Orthodox denominations; she called it fatherly protection, others unwanted interference.

The result was a delay for the Balkan nations in acquiring their full independence. Not farther back than 1835, A. W. Kinglake writes in his *Eothen*: "Though the province of Serbia generally has obtained a kind of independence, yet Belgrade, as being a place of strength on the frontier, is still garrisoned by Turkish troops under the command of a Pasha." After 1860 Michael Obrenovič had the pluck to abolish this last measure. And in a widely comprehensive outlook he came to view the necessity of an approach and understanding not only of the Serbs, but of all who were carrying the burden of oppression in the Balkans. Commenting on such an aim,

Rebecca West in the *Black Lamb and Grey Falcon* with much warm sympathy, as one would have expected from her, adds: " A check was sharply applied to his plan when England and France, with incredible fatuity, joined Austria-Hungary in rebuking him. It is difficult to imagine why they did this." The reason might be found, I think, in the words uttered by Lady Macduff—Shakespeare's Macbeth:

> *I am in the earthly world, where to do harm*
> *Is often laudable, to do good sometime*
> *Accounted dangerous folly. . . .*

It was indeed a " dangerous folly " for Michael Obrenovič, so Austria-Hungary considered, to upset her interests, whilst for the sake of their own interests the other Great Powers had to mind the interests of Austria-Hungary. It seemed too a " dangerous folly " on the part of Rhiga Pheraios to go counter to the designs of Austria-Hungary by forming a Balkan union. That is why he was handed over by the Austro-Hungarian authorities to the Belgrade executioners.

The frontiers of the Balkan states expanded or shrank according to the whims and influences at the time of one or other of the Great Powers. At the Treaty of San Stefano there had been allotted to the Bulgarians a tremendous excess of territory. Bulgaria herself felt in a state of bursting, like the swollen creature of the fable. Something unclean hung in the atmosphere after San Stefano. One sensed a strong suspicion, and one hurried to undo the work of that Treaty by a new congress in Berlin, where only representatives of the Great Powers gathered. What could one say ? In a simple expression, theirs was the bread and theirs was the knife, so they cut it as they pleased, as it better served their own end. They did not mind at all the future, they did not realize that any wrongs done do not pass in oblivion; they smoulder like stagnant waters and breed poisonous miasma of unrest that affect, not only the wronged people, but also those through whom the wrongs were created.

One has to recognize that real representatives of the English thought and tradition, such as Gladstone and Lord Salisbury, did not fail to raise their voices in defence of the small nations, who were then cast altogether at the mercy of greedily unassuaged monsters.

For a long time before the Congress of Berlin some of the Great Powers pleased themselves to pursue a sinister game in the Danubian provinces, until the governing classes of the latter came to their senses: " Why should we, sons of the same nation, live apart and not pull up together in a single Rumanian state ?"

Do you suppose this harmless Christian desire was approved by the majority of the Great Powers ? No, they thought it was better for those provinces to be separated. But in spite of them, when one found strength in oneself, in the deep, unsuspected vital sources of the people, and one declared the union with full rights of sovereignty, the Great Powers resigned themselves into accepting it. They said about Rumania as they did about a single free Bulgaria and the rest of the Balkan states: " Independence they want ? Let them be independent ! But in so far as they remain dependent on us." And they kept to this device, which assumed more importance since in one or other of the countries some of the God-vouchsafed riches in the shape of minerals, oil, and such like were brought to light. Then it came to pass that the old story of the Bible had again to be faced: " Naboth the Jezreelite had a vineyard, which was in Jezreel, hard by the palace of Ahab, King of Samaria. And Ahab spake unto Naboth saying, ' Give me thy vineyard.' . . ."

Maybe the Great Powers were prompted not only by interest. They had also a desire to help. But there is a rough saying among the Vlachs, " A foreigner scratches you where you do not itch." In order to do the scratching, the Great Powers divided the Balkans into spheres of influence; and, as this expression savoured too much of past troubles, it was occasionally replaced by calling the Balkan States satellites moving in the orbit of one or the other of the Great Powers, who alone were able to radiate a beneficent light.

How the Balkan States reacted and how events unfolded themselves down to our own days I shall not relate, for I am not concerned with the present; my aim here is that of Thucydides in *The Peloponnesian War*, to give " a true knowledge of the past in order to interpret the future," if one ever cares for such an interpretation.

BIBLIOGRAPHY

Rebecca West, *Black Lamb and Grey Falcon*, Vol. 1, London, 1940.

C. Fauriel, *Chants Populaires de la Grèce Moderne*, Tome 1, Paris.

Marcu Beza, *Paganism in Rumanian Folklore*, London, 1928.

R. A. S. Macalister, *A Century of Excavations in Palestine*, 1925.

Moses Gaster, *Literatura Populară Română*, Bucuresti, 1883.

Steven Runciman, *The Emperor Romanus Lecapenus and his Reign*, Cambridge, 1929.

J. F. Abbot, *The Tales of a Tour in Macedonia*, London, 1903.

Marcu Beza, *Byzantine Art in Rumania*, Messrs. B. T. Batsford, Ltd., London, 1940.

B. Filov: *L'Art Antique en Bulgarie*, Paris, 1922.

Marcu Beza, *The Rumanian Church*, S.P.C.K., 1943.
    For the Byzantine idea of seeing the Balkan people as a collectivity.
    B. Matranga, *Anecdota Græca*, p. 677, and *Epirotica*, ed. Bonn, p. 238.

Passow, *Popularia Carmina Græca*, Lipsiæ, 1860.

August Dozon, *Chansons Populaires Bulgares*, Paris, 1875.

William Hareborne account is given in *Richard Hakluyt*, the second volume of the *Principal Navigations, Voyages, Traffiques, and Discoveries of the English Nation*, ed. 1599, p. 426.

Lord Paget's letters in the Record Office, State Papers, *Turkey*, Vol. XX.

Edmund Chishull, *Travels in Turkey and Back to England*, London, 1747.

INDEX

*Printed in Great Britain by
Billing and Sons Ltd., Guildford and Esher*
F5833